An Introduction

MARKE I
& SOCIAL
RESEARCH

Planning & using research tools & techniques

Karen Adams *&* **Ian Brace**

London and Philadelphia

This book is dedicated to our families, and to all the staff at MRS – especially Sam, Hayley, Michelle and Harriet.

Publisher's note

Every possible effort has been made to ensure that the information contained in this book is accurate at the time of going to press, and the publishers and authors cannot accept responsibility for any errors or omissions, however caused. No responsibility for loss or damage occasioned to any person acting, or refraining from action, as a result of the material in this publication can be accepted by the editor, the publisher or the authors.

First published in Great Britain and the United States in 2006 by Kogan Page Limited

120 Pentonville Road
London N1 9JN
United Kingdom
www.kogan-page.co.uk

525 South 4th Street, #241
Philadelphia PA 19147
USA

© Karen Adams and Ian Brace, 2006

The right of Karen Adams and Ian Brace to be identified as the author of this work has been asserted by them in accordance with the Copyright, Designs and Patents Act 1988.

ISBN 0 7494 4377 4

British Library Cataloguing-in-Publication Data

A CIP record for this book is available from the British Library.

Library of Congress Cataloging-in-Publication Data

Adams, Karen.
   An introduction to market and social research : planning and using research tools and techniques / Karen Adams and Ian Brace.
       p. cm.
   ISBN 0-7494-4377-4
   1. Marketing research. I. Brace, Ian. II. Title.
   HF5415.2.A17 2006
   658.8'3--dc22

                                                                                        2006023957

Typeset by Saxon Graphics Ltd, Derby
Printed and bound in Great Britain by Bell & Bain, Glasgow

Contents

Acknowledgements

Many thanks to everyone who helped us while the book was in progress. In particular, we would like to thank Frances Yelland for her guidance on qualitative analysis, Anne Dobbin and Angela Hildreth for their hours of work and Kogan Page editor Jon Finch for making things happen. Thanks, too, to Debrah Harding, Yvonne McGivern and Marianne Hough for their helpful feedback. And, last but definitely not least, thanks to Simon Williams for his patience and support, and his expert help.

The MRS/City & Guilds Examination

The examination for the MRS/City & Guilds Certificate comprises 40 multiple-choice questions, many of which focus on your knowledge of key terms and concepts. To support your preparation for the examination, key terms have been highlighted in the text using bold *italics*. Use the terminology test at the end of each chapter to test your knowledge of these terms. If you would like more information, visit the glossary of Market Research Terms on the MRS website (www.mrs.org.uk).

For more information on the MRS/City& Guilds Certificate in Market & Social Research Practice, visit www.mrs.org.uk

How to use this book

An Introduction to Market and Social Research provides a step-by-step guide to the research process, from the identification of the topic to be researched to the delivery of results and recommendations. It combines clear explanations and practical examples to guide you through the decisions that need to be made at each stage in the research process.

The book follows the syllabus of the MRS/City & Guilds Certificate in Market and Social Research, and provides tasks and tests to help you prepare for the examination for this qualification in the following ways:

- The book is divided into three sections, mirroring the syllabus of the MRS/City & Guilds Certificate.

- Each chapter contains:
  - a clear description of what you will learn in the chapter;
  - clear explanations and practical examples to help you understand key points;
  - a series of tasks to help you apply what you are learning to practical situations, with suggested answers provided in an answer guide;
  - a terminology revision test to help ensure that you remember key terms and concepts in market and social research.

- Throughout the book, you will have the chance to apply what you are learning to an unfolding market research case study.

- The final section includes a series of exam-type questions to help you test your knowledge and prepare for the MRS/City& Guild Certificate examination.

Introduction to market research

Why do I need research?

Introducing market and social research

Introduction

The results of research are all around us. If you watch the news, or read newspapers or magazines, you are likely to see or hear the words 'a study shows ...', 'a new survey indicates ...' or 'people aged between 25 and 35 are likely to ...'. Behind each of these statements lie research findings. However, how did the process of research begin? And how did it reach its conclusions?

In this chapter, you will learn how to:

- define and describe 'market research';
- explain why organizations use market research;
- identify how the market research industry is structured;
- describe some of the key work roles within market research;
- describe the ethical and legal frameworks which govern market research.

What *is* 'market research'?

All organizations, whether they are commercial companies, not-for-profit organizations or public sector bodies, need to develop and change. However, deciding how best to change can be a complex task. For example, if a charity wants to find new ways of raising funds, it needs to look at the various options open to it and try to select the one which will be most effective. To make this decision, the organization needs information: which option is likely to bring in most money? How will potential donors respond to this new way of raising funds? What are the risks involved in raising funds in this new way? All of this information can help the charity to consider its options carefully, and to make the most appropriate choice. And this is where market research plays a key role. Well-planned and well-executed research can provide the accurate and relevant information needed to help the organization make its business decision.

Defining 'research'

The Market Research Society (MRS) is the world's largest professional body for individuals working in, or interested in, market, social and opinion research. It defines research as:

> the collection and analysis of data from a sample or census of individuals or organizations relating to their characteristics, behaviour, attitudes, opinions or possessions.

(MRS, 2005: 6)

As the MRS definition demonstrates, researchers gather information from people and organizations about all aspects of their lives: what they think, what they do, how they spend their money. How this information is used will depend on the reasons for undertaking the research project. A local council that needs to decide how to prioritize its spending might consult local residents to find out their views. A holiday company seeking to expand its list of holiday destinations might need to find out which possible destinations most interest potential customers. In all cases, it is the organization's *business problem* that dictates what information will be gathered. By identifying what decisions need to be made, the researcher can work out what information is needed.

Using research to inform business decisions

As the examples above demonstrate, research can be used to help identify possible solutions to a wide range of problems. In essence, any business decision can be informed by effective research. However, there are some key business areas that depend heavily on research.

■ **Developing new products.** Developing and launching a new product or service can be a very expensive venture, and a business needs to know that it has a good chance of being successful. Carrying out research at different stages in the development process can help identify best choices and possible problems.

- **Understanding how brands are performing.** In an environment where different brands compete for the same share of the market, it's important that companies understand how well their brand is doing. Through research, the company will be able to understand its brand's areas of strength, and identify areas where competitors are beginning to overtake it.

- **Segmenting the market.** Organizations in all sectors – commercial companies, government agencies and not-for-profit organizations – deal with a very wide range of people. This means that the organization's customers or contacts could have very diverse needs. By *segmenting* their market – that is, by identifying different sub-groups within their group of customers – organizations can tailor their services to the needs of those different groups. For example, a local library might know that the majority of its members are adults aged 45+. However, there might also be a significant number of teenagers and of younger children who use the library. By identifying these different segments, the library can develop to meet the needs of all of the different groups of members.

- **Communicating with customers.** Organizations can now make contact with their customers using a huge variety of media: email, the internet and television advertising are only a few. But how can the organization know which approach is most effective? Research plays a major role in assessing the effectiveness of advertising and other forms of communication between organizations and their customers.

- **Gauging how satisfied customers are.** One important feature of a successful organization is that it retains customers as well as gaining new ones. Being able to find out how customers feel about the services or products an organization provides is vital to retaining their loyalty and custom. Measuring customer satisfaction is now a major area of research for a wide range of organizations, from colleges which ask students to complete evaluation forms, through to restaurants and hotels where guests are asked to complete a short questionnaire when they visit.

In some organizations, research is carried out occasionally when a business problem or issue is identified, while in others research is carried out on a continual basis. An example of this can be seen in major retailers and owners of big brands, which need to be constantly aware of how their brand is faring against the competition.

Market research and social research: the same or different?

MRS is a professional body whose members include individuals who work either in market research or in social research. But what is the difference between the two?

Market research is very much a commercial activity, focused on gathering information to help the organization address a business problem.

Social research focuses on gathering information about society and social issues. In many cases, this information is needed to help make a decision. An example is research to help a health authority measure the effectiveness of an anti-smoking campaign. However, social research is also carried out with the aim of helping us to understand society more fully. The information might be used to inform decisions at a later date, but the primary aim might have been simply to further understanding of the subject area.

Although the aims of projects may differ, both market and social research are based on the same principles and share many techniques. There is now a greater crossover than before between the two disciplines, with many market research suppliers carrying out both market and social research.

In this book, we will be looking at research as it is used to help solve business problems. Importantly, however, those problems may be set in commercial contexts or in social contexts. To find out more about social research, visit the MRS website and the website of the Social Research Association, a membership organization in the UK specifically for social researchers (www.the-sra.org.UK).

Who carries out research?

We often hear that a major organization has launched a new product or decided to open offices in a new area. But how does the organization gather the information required to help make those decisions?

The client and the supplier

In most market research projects, there are two key roles: the client and the supplier.

The *client* is the person, the department or the organization that needs the research information. The *research supplier* is commissioned by the client to carry out the research on its behalf, and to provide guidance to help the client understand the research results.

Larger companies or organizations may have their own internal research team which is commissioned to carry out research. However, these teams of *clientside researchers* tend to be relatively small, and a project might need a larger research team. When the company is unable to carry out its own research, it normally enlists the services of an external research supplier, in the form of either an individual research consultant or a larger research agency.

How research agencies are structured

Within the UK, market research is a multi-million pound industry sector, and a wide range of research agencies exists, many specializing in specific research areas. Clients normally select agencies based on their expertise either in one particular type of research, or in their work with different types of clients or in different countries.

As with most industry sectors, the UK market research sector includes agencies of different sizes, some with only a few staff and others which are global organizations with offices in many countries. Some may offer only a limited range of research services, while others (known as *full-service agencies*) carry out all aspects of the research process. So who works in a full-service agency, and what do they do? Although there is a wide range of agencies, all of which might be structured slightly differently, there are some standard ways in which a project might be delegated to different staff members. Table 1.1 shows how a research project often includes people from a wide range of departments.

In many cases, client companies work with a limited number of research suppliers. This helps build relationships in which the client is sure that the researchers understand the context in which the client works, and recognize the importance of the business problem. However, other clients work with a wide range of suppliers. In all cases, the research supplier – either agency or consultant – needs to demonstrate that it has the understanding, skills and experience to address the research problem appropriately. In order to do

Table 1.1 *People involved in research*

Where do they work?	Research department		Operations department	
Who are they?	Director/associate director (very experienced researchers)	Senior research executive/research executive (less experienced researchers)	Field department (interviewers, supervisors and field managers)	Data processing department (data analysts and other staff responsible for electronic handling of data)
What do they do?	Usually responsible for meeting with the client and deciding on the parameters of the research project. Ensuring the success of the project is the responsibility of the staff at this level.	Usually responsible for carrying out the more detailed aspects of the project, such as designing the questionnaire, and the day-to-day management of the project. Staff at this level may also be involved in presenting the findings of the research to the client.	Usually responsible for gathering data from the *respondents*, ie the individuals who agree to participate in the research	Usually responsible for the entering, editing and running analysis of data

this, the supplier will normally produce a research proposal to demonstrate how it will address the problem. Clients may invite a number of agencies or consultants to submit proposals and select the one that most closely fits their needs. In Chapter 2, we look at how such proposals are put together.

Researching the research agencies

The *Research Buyer's Guide (RBG)*, the UK's largest directory of research suppliers, is produced annually by MRS. It includes a wide range of agencies and consultants, with details of the types of research they carry out, the numbers of staff they employ, and where they operate in the world.

The online version of RBG can be searched to find agencies by size, region, research type and area of business. To find out more about agencies operating in your area, visit www.rbg.org.uk

Conducting research ethically

As we saw at the beginning of this chapter, research is carried out on behalf of a wide range of organizations. In some cases, the organization will be seeking information from individual members of the public. An example is when a research interviewer stops a person in the street and asks him or her to participate in some research. In other cases, the organization might need to find out what other businesses or organizations think or do: for example, an IT supplier might need to find out how a business uses IT in order to be able to market its products to that business. This type of research, known as *business-to-business research*, can help businesses understand each other more effectively. In all cases, however, the people providing the information – the respondents – need to be sure that their views are being represented accurately, and that the details they provide are kept secure.

Because market research depends heavily on gathering information about people, it is important that a clear ethical framework exists – and is seen to exist – to protect the rights of respondents. In the UK, MRS is the regulator of ethical standards in market research. The regulations in the **MRS Code of Conduct** govern all aspects of the research process, including the rights of respondents. All members of MRS, and the companies they work for, are bound by this Code. Some of the key underpinning principles of the Code of Conduct include:

■ **The need to gain *informed consent* from a respondent.** Before respondents can be asked to provide information, they must understand what will be done with the information. The purpose of the research also needs to be made clear to the respondent before any interview can take place.

- **The right to anonymity.** Effective research depends on the respondent feeling comfortable enough to share information. In many cases, respondents would be unwilling to participate in research if they felt their identity was to be made known to the client. As a result, respondents should be assured that their identity will be protected. In some cases, the researcher may need to include the respondent's name or other details in any analysis of the data. If this is the case, specific permission needs to be sought from the respondent during the interview.

- **Information should be treated as confidential.** As well as being anonymous, respondents have the right to expect that their views will be treated as confidential. This is particularly important when researching sensitive areas. An example is a survey of employee satisfaction in a company. If the survey is to find out exactly what employees think of the company, the employees must be sure that the views they express will not be traced back to them. Researchers need to ensure that the views of the individual are kept confidential, and that it is only the views of the group that are fed back to the client. They can only pass back information that could identify an individual with the express permission of that individual.

- **Data is held in accordance with data protection legislation.** In the UK, the 1998 Data Protection Act gives individuals certain rights over information that is held about them. One of the foremost principles in the Act is that information about an individual must not be passed on to a third party without his or her approval. The MRS Code of Conduct, and associated guidelines, help interpret the Act as it relates to market research information.

- **No one will try to sell respondents anything as a result of their taking part.** Market research has nothing to do with selling anything directly to the people who take part in the research. Members of the public would not cooperate if they thought it was just an excuse to sell them something.

MRS, and the research profession in general, take the rights of respondents very seriously. It is recognized that if people are not confident that their information will be handled properly, they are unlikely to participate in research. One of the key roles of the researcher, then, is to ensure that all the work he or she does is carried out in line with the MRS Code of Conduct.

The MRS Code of Conduct, along with the guidelines produced by MRS to help researchers ensure ethical practice, can be downloaded from the MRS website (www.mrs.org.uk/standards).

Becoming research aware: practical task

While you are reading this book, try to become more aware of the research going on around you. To do this, look for instances of research projects in newspapers or in the news. Key words to look out for include:

■ survey;

■ study;

■ research;

■ statistics.

When you find an example of a research project, try to answer the following questions:

1. Who is the client?

2. Who is the research supplier? You may find this information on a graph or diagram.

3. What was the problem that needed research?

4. What was the outcome of the research?

If you identify the research supplier, try to find out more about it by visiting the RBG website (www.rbg.org.uk) or by looking for it on the net, using a search engine.

Terminology test

The following research terms were introduced in this chapter. Can you explain what each one means?

■ market research

■ segmentation

■ research supplier

■ respondent

■ MRS Code of Conduct

■ client

■ clientside researcher

■ business-to-business

Summary

Some of the key points from this chapter are:

- 'Market research' involves the gathering of information from individuals and organizations in order to aid business decision making.

- Research is normally commissioned by a client and carried out by a supplier. However, don't forget that the client and the supplier may work for the same organization.

- Much of the research undertaken in the UK is carried out by research agencies. Different agencies specialize in different types of research or research for specific sectors.

- The MRS Code of Conduct provides the regulatory framework for research carried out in the UK. All members of the MRS are bound by the Code, wherever they are working.

What do I need to know?

Defining research objectives

Introduction

All businesses and organizations need to find ways to develop in order to meet the demands of a changing environment. For example, an organization may want to measure how its business is progressing, to improve on the products or services it offers, or to expand into a new area. In each case, effective research can provide the guidance and support needed for the organization to make business decisions.

In this chapter, you will learn how to:

- explore the background to a business 'problem';
- define the research 'problem';
- identify research objectives;
- identify the resources needed for a research project;
- create an effective research brief.

The first steps

Before a research project can begin, there are a number of important steps that must be taken. It is vital that the research is based on a clear understanding of the problem the information might help solve. As a result, the client and the researcher may spend some time discussing the possible research requirement, even before a formal research brief is written. Therefore, the steps described in this chapter may develop as a cycle, with problems being analysed and refined, rather than proceed as a sequence.

What is the problem?

As we saw in Chapter 1, research findings play an important role in informing decision making in business and organizations. They provide evidence which can be used to help solve a business problem or challenge.

Business problems in practice: case study

T H Stores is a small, family-owned supermarket in a residential area of a large town. The owners opened the shop 10 years ago, and the business is doing well. Encouraged by this success, they are now interested in expanding their business. They are considering either enlarging their current shop or opening another shop in a different area of town.

This is their *business problem* – how can they expand their business? Any research undertaken needs to provide information that can help them address this problem.

From problem to objectives

Once the business problem or goal has been identified, the business or organization may need additional information about its potential choices to help make the final decision. It is at this point that the research process begins. The first stage in any research project is to define precisely the research problem. This problem definition is usually achieved by the researcher talking with the client to find out what exactly needs to be researched. In order to identify the research problem, a number of important questions need to be answered:

- **What is known already?** It is important to investigate the background to the business problem. Understanding the business context will help the researcher identify precisely which areas need to be researched. The first step, therefore, is to ask questions about:
  - *The business*. It is important to understand the business or organization – its history and how it is structured – in order to understand the context of the business problem. Knowing about the aims of the organization, its clients and its current products or services will help the researcher to develop a wider understanding of the circumstances that gave rise to the business problem.
  - *The wider environment*. Businesses and organizations do not operate in isolation. All need to be aware of their competitors or any changes in the social or political

landscape which might affect how they do business. The researcher may be able to draw on previous research to gain this type of insight. For example, if a local council wishes to introduce a new scheme to recycle household waste, it might be possible to find out if other councils have already started similar schemes, and how successful these have been. This type of information can help to identify the areas that need to be researched further.

■ **What decisions need to be made?** The researcher needs to understand the client's business problem, and to see how research findings will inform the decision-making process. This will help identify precisely the area that needs to be researched.

■ **Is the research really possible?** In some circumstances, it may not be possible to carry out the research the client wants. There might be ethical, financial or time constraints which mean that it simply is not possible to gather the information which is asked for. Remember that it is important to identify any restrictions that exist when identifying the research problem.

A thorough understanding of the background and the business problem is vital to the research project. Without this understanding, the researcher might not identify exactly what needs to be researched, and therefore the research project will not provide the information which is required. Identifying constraints will help the researcher avoid setting unrealistic or unachievable aims for the project.

Once the research problem has been identified, it needs to be broken down further into a series of *research objectives*. Research objectives identify exactly the areas or topics that need to be investigated, and are usually set out as questions. For example, if a gym is investigating ways of attracting new members, the research objectives might include:

■ How does this gym compare with others in the area?

■ What do current members think of the gym?

■ Why did former members leave?

■ What might encourage members of other gyms to move to this one?

In some cases, a research objective may take the form of a *hypothesis* to be investigated. For example, a train company might want to know if people are more likely to use commuter trains in poor weather than when it is fine. Its research hypothesis would be 'Passenger numbers on commuter trains are related to changes in the weather'.

Research objectives in practice: case study

The owners of T H Stores have decided to expand the business but need to be sure that the option they choose will bring a good return. The cheaper option is to enlarge the current store. However, they are worried that, by enlarging, they might lose the family-friendly environment they currently have, which they think has been an important factor in their current success. They need to know more about the possible impact of enlarging their store on their current customers, and if their investment would pay off in increased sales.

T H Stores' business problem is, 'What is the best way to expand?' The research problem, however, is narrower than the business problem. In fact, if the owners seriously wish to consider two options, they have two separate research problems: one that focuses on enlargement of the current store and one that focuses on setting up a new store. If they want to take the first option, they need to find out 'how customers might respond to an enlarged store'. This broad research problem can be broken down into a number of objectives:

■ Who are the customers (ages, where they live, etc)?

■ Why do customers choose to shop here?

■ What range of goods do they buy here?

■ Where else do they shop, and why?

■ Would an enlarged shop encourage them to spend more here?

Finding resources for the research project

Before embarking on a research project, it's important to identify the resources you have – and the resources you need – to undertake the project. This will help to avoid making over-ambitious plans, and ensure that the project can meet the aims set for it. The following checklist highlights the questions that need to be answered when considering resources.

■ **Who will do the research?** In most business situations, the client will commission researchers to carry out the project. These researchers may work for an external research supplier, or could be members of a different department within the client's company. Sometimes, however, the client and the researcher will be the same person. This might happen in a small organization or business, where no separate budget exists for research and the project becomes part of the 'client's' workload. It is important to recognize, however, that this approach may have substantial hidden costs, particularly if the project has to be fitted into an already busy schedule.

■ **How much information is required?** When a research project is planned, it can be tempting to try to gather information about a wide range of issues that are not directly relevant to the research problem. Don't forget that asking for more information than is needed can result in increased costs and a longer deadline for the delivery of results.

- ▧ **What is the deadline for the project?** It is not uncommon for businesses or organizations to expect results within a very short time. However, short deadlines can result in research being rushed or findings limited. It's important that any deadline gives enough time for each step of the research process to be completed fully so that the researcher and the client can be sure that the findings are accurate and relevant to the business problem.

- ▧ **How much money is available for the project?** It's important to set aside a reasonable budget for the project. The amount of money available will, obviously, depend on the size of the organization, the in-house resources available and the extent of the problem being researched. Remember, however, that spending money on research may help the company or organization save money in the long term.

When the resources have been identified, the client can start the research process by creating a research brief.

Creating the research brief

The *research brief* provides the basis for the research project. The brief, which is usually written but may take the form of a discussion between a client and a researcher, gives the parameters of the research required: the problem, the reason for the research, and the resources available.

A well-written brief can provide a great deal of support to help the researcher create a suitable *research proposal*, showing exactly how the research project will be carried out. To be most effective, the brief should contain the following sections:

- ▧ **History of the business/organization.** This background information is important to help the researcher understand the context of the problem. This section may not be necessary if the researcher comes from inside the client's company.

- ▧ **Background to the problem.** As was shown above, accurate and relevant background information can help the researcher to refine the research problem.

- ▧ **The reason for the research.** Why does the client need the information? What decisions need to be made? Including this information will allow the researcher to identify whether the client has diagnosed the research problem accurately, or additional questions need to be asked.

- ▧ **What will be done with the information.** The client may need to publish the results or present the findings of the research to an international meeting. This information will help the researcher identify the 'deliverables' – the forms in which the information needs to be delivered. This might include a full written report, a presentation at board level, or via video conferencing. Including this section will enable the researcher to include the 'deliverables' in the costing.

■ **The deadline for delivery of the findings.** A clear indication of timing is needed to ensure that the project designed matches the time available.

■ **The budget.** The amount of money available will dictate the methods the researcher can use, and how the money will be allocated at different stages in the project.

Once the brief has been prepared, the researcher can begin to design a project to meet the client's needs. If the client is commissioning research from an external supplier it might invite several research agencies to send in proposals, and select the one it thinks is best.

Creating a research brief: practice tasks

Good research briefs provide enough background information to allow the researcher to fully understand the context and the business problem. This background information can be drawn from a wide variety of sources, including:

■ the business's financial records;

■ its range of clients;

■ information about its existing market, or its main competitors;

■ information taken from previous research projects.

Example

The owners of T H Stores want to know if it is advisable to enlarge their current store. The background information they could supply includes:

■ information about their financial situation – how profitable the store has been since it opened;

■ who the customers are, and when the store is most busy and quiet;

■ what the most popular lines are, for example whether customers buy general goods, or specific types of goods;

■ information on the possibility of extending the store, such as whether the owners own adjacent property or have planning permission for an extension;

■ whether there are any other supermarkets nearby, or any plans for major new developments.

Look at the following research problems. In each case, try to identify what background information could be included in the brief to help the researcher understand the business problem:

■ The owner of a small restaurant wants to start selling her own brand of homemade sauces in specialist food shops.

■ A local council wants residents to recycle more of their household waste.

■ An electronics company wants to move into a new overseas market.

See page 137 for a list of suggestions.

Terminology test

The following research terms were introduced in this chapter. Can you explain what each one means?

■ research objectives   ■ hypothesis

■ research brief   ■ research proposal

Summary

■ Remember that research will be used to help the client make a business decision. Understanding the business problem is an important first step.

■ Effective research depends on well-defined objectives. Make sure that the objectives are based on a clear analysis of the client's business problem and information needs.

■ Don't forget to consider resources at an early stage. Identifying the resources available will help set the parameters for the research.

■ The research brief can be a formal written document produced by the client, or can develop in discussion between the client and researcher. Whichever form it takes, it should provide the range of information a researcher needs to develop a proposal.

■ A good researcher will challenge the client's brief, reanalyse the problems and, if necessary, redefine the research objectives to make sure that the project produces the information the client needs. As a result, time spent discussing the problem before the research project is designed can bring important benefits to the finished research design.

How am I going to do it?

Selecting a research design

Introduction

When planning a research project, it's important to be aware of the range of research options that exists, and to choose the one that is most suitable for the research problem.

In this chapter, you will learn how to:

■ identify a range of different types of research;

■ choose the research design that is most appropriate for a given research problem;

■ start to structure an effective research proposal.

Defining information needs

Choosing the right *research design* is vital if your project is going to provide the information that is needed. To find the right design, think about the four following questions:

■ Does the information already exist, or do I have to discover it for the first time?

■ Does the client need facts and figures, or opinions and feelings – or both types of information?

■ Should the research explore new areas, get reactions to a new idea, describe what is known already, or identify cause and effect?

■ Do I want to find out about a trend over time, or take a single 'snapshot' of the situation at one point in time?

The answer to each question will take you closer to the research design you need.

Does the information already exist, or do I have to discover it for the first time?

It might be possible to identify a lot of information that is relevant to your research simply by reading. You might be able to find the answers to your research questions by drawing together information from a wide range of sources such as:

■ existing research reports;

■ the organization's own records and materials;

■ competitors' websites;

■ journals and magazines.

This type of research, where the researcher looks for relevant information that already exists, is called *secondary research* or *desk research*. By gathering together this information and reviewing it against the research objectives, you may find that some of your research questions have already been answered.

However, you may need to talk to a range of different people to find the information you need. For example, to find out what consumers think about a new product, you will need to talk directly with those consumers. *Primary research* uncovers information for the first time. There are a number of ways of gathering this information, with the most common being through interviews and questionnaires, and through observing people in action.

Many research projects begin with secondary research, then move on to a phase of primary research in order to answer any questions that remain.

'Primary' and 'secondary' describe where we *find* information. However, it's also important to identify the *type* of information that is needed.

Primary or secondary? Practice task

In Chapter 2, you thought about the research brief for a local council that wants to encourage residents to recycle more. Below is a list of different research activities the council could carry out. In each case, decide whether the researcher is doing primary research or secondary research:

1. Searching the internet for reports on recycling in other towns or areas.

2. Interviewing residents to find out what type of waste they recycle.

3. Counting the number of people who visit the council's recycling centre on one day.

4. Calculating how much was recycled in the council's area last year, using council records.

5. Identifying the different types of waste recycled by visiting the recycling centre.

6. Contacting councils whose reports you found on the internet in order to speak with them about their programmes.

Compare your answers with those on page 138.

Does the client need facts and figures, or opinions and feelings – or both types of information?

This question lies at the heart of a research project, and represents a traditional division in research. *Quantitative research* aims to quantify responses and information. Questions in quantitative studies usually ask for responses that can be counted in some way, such as yes/no answers or scales from 1 to 5. The resulting information can be expressed as statistics. For example, a quantitative report may show the percentage of people who agree or disagree with a particular statement or question, or use graphs to illustrate its findings.

However, the client might need to understand what motivates people to behave in a certain way, or why they hold certain opinions. This might be particularly important, for example, when a company wants to launch a brand new product. It might need to find out what people think of the product before it can find out how many think in this way. *Qualitative research* aims to uncover information about the way people think and behave, and to identify patterns in those thoughts and behaviours. Importantly, qualitative studies gather information using open-ended questions and recording the responses word for word, or by watching how people respond in different situations. The people being interviewed express their thoughts in the way they wish, and the researcher's role is to evaluate the importance and relevance of what is said and done.

Although it is easy to see quantitative and qualitative research as opposing approaches – one measuring responses and reactions, the other exploring them in more depth – many projects require both types of information. For example, a train operator that wants to make savings might need to find out which routes are least used. It therefore needs to have figures for the number of passengers on its various services, and which routes are the least profitable. But it might also have to consider the impact that cutting less-profitable services could have on passengers. It might be that cutting the services would have a negative impact on the way the public views the company – and this could affect its business. To find this out, the researcher might have to talk directly with those passengers and explore their experiences and opinions.

In many research projects, a qualitative stage is included near the beginning to establish the range of opinions you might expect to find around one area. These can provide the basis for a quantitative stage, where the researcher tries to establish how many of these views are shared by a large number of people. For example, a newspaper that is considering changing its size and look might ask a small group of readers for their opinions. The researcher might then identify the most common opinions and create a questionnaire to find out how many of the newspaper's readers think the same.

It is important that the questions in the quantitative stage are phrased in a way that respondents easily understand. Often, one of the roles of a qualitative stage is to determine the words that people use when thinking about the product. These words can then be used in the questionnaire, rather than the different and perhaps more technical words that the manufacturer uses.

Quantitative or qualitative information? Practice task

In Chapter 2, you read about T H Stores' plans to enlarge its current supermarket. The research objectives for its research project are shown below. For each one, try to identify the type of information that is needed – quantitative or qualitative?

T H Stores Research Project: Research Objectives

1. Who are the customers (ages, where they live, etc)?

2. Why do customers choose to shop here?

3. What range of goods do they buy here?

4. Where else do they shop, and why?

5. Would an enlarged shop encourage them to spend more here?

Compare your answers with those on page 138.

It's important to realize that both quantitative and qualitative information may have an important role to play in a project. The job of the researcher is to identify exactly what each type of information can bring to the project, and which type is needed first.

Should the research explore new areas, get reactions to a new idea, describe what is known already, or identify cause and effect?

The type of information a researcher needs will often be dictated by how much is already known, and what the client wants to do with the information. The newspaper owners might be at the very beginning of the process of changing their newspaper. At this stage, they may have no idea about how their readers will react, and they may only want to explore the possible reactions to the changes. An *exploratory research design* allows the researcher to do this. Exploratory research projects are carried out to gather initial observations, feelings and reactions, and often to provide the basis for further research. They often rely on the gathering of qualitative information and this, in turn, will show if the idea is worth following up.

Other research studies may simply need to record the situation as it is. Many social research studies are designed to do this. A national census, for example, gathers information about the number of people living in a country: who they are, what they do, how many people live in each house and so on. The aim of the census is to describe the country at the time the survey is carried out. This *descriptive research* paints a very clear picture of a situation, and is therefore useful in establishing what is real, rather than assumed. Descriptive research designs often use quantitative methods to establish the facts about a situation.

A third important type of research study includes those designed to find out about the impact one thing has on another. For example, the owners of a sandwich bar might assume that cold weather will increase demand for hot sandwiches or soup. *Causal research* will help them to work out if their hypothesis – that cold weather causes an increase in demand for hot food – is true. The aim of causal research is to find out if there is a real link between two variables. In the case of the sandwich bar owners, they want to find out if a change to colder weather really does cause their customers to buy more hot food, or if the change they have noticed only happened by chance. Many other variables – such as customers wanting to change their diet, or being bored with the usual selection of sandwiches – might influence their buying habits. However, research can help identify if the link between cold weather and hot food is particularly strong. Knowing this could help the sandwich bar owners increase their sales by identifying the best times to offer more hot food.

Exploring, describing or testing links? Practice task

Look at the following research problems. In each case, decide if the required research design should be exploratory, descriptive or causal.

1. A local college wants to open a new department, offering business courses for local businesses. However, the college principal does not know if any other colleges in the area are offering similar courses. This information is vital, as too much competition could cause the courses to fail.

2. A company that owns a chain of gyms wants to know if people who want to lose weight should be advised to join an exercise class, or have a series of one-to-one classes with a personal trainer. This information will help it plan its autumn fitness classes.

3. A local council wants to know if its area has more or less crime than the national average. It has the national crime figures for the previous year for comparison.

4. A mobile phone company is thinking about producing a new style of phone for elderly people, with larger numbers and easy-to-use text features. However, the company needs to know how people would react to this innovation. Currently, all of its research has been into developing more hi-tech options.

Compare your answers with those on pages 138–39.

As well as deciding what type of information you need, you also have to consider when and how often you collect the information.

Do I want to find out about a trend over time, or take a single 'snapshot' of the situation at one point in time?

When deciding on the timeframe of a research project, it's important to consider two questions. Do you need to find out about the situation at a single point in time, or over a longer period? And do you need to speak to the respondents only once, or a number of times? The answers to these questions will provide the final element of your research design.

Many research projects are designed to investigate a single problem at a single point in time. These *ad hoc* projects investigate problems that require an almost immediate answer: for example, the newspaper owners we discussed earlier need to know now if they should make the changes they plan. An ad hoc project is one that investigates a research problem once only, with the research designed specifically to answer that problem and no other. The type of research design that gathers information from a wide range of sources on one occasion is known as *cross-sectional research*. Although an ad hoc project might take a few weeks, or in some cases months, to complete, the information from cross-sectional research provides the researcher and the client with a 'snapshot' of the situation at one point in time. The researcher cannot promise that if he or she were to go back to do the same project next year, he or she would find the same results.

Cross-sectional research is vital for many business problems: clients often need to know if *now* is the right time to make changes or launch a new product. However, other types of business problems require more long-term projects. A television station, for example, might need to know how many viewers watch its programmes in comparison with a rival station. However, what viewers watch might vary over time – for example, the rival station might launch new programmes which change viewing behaviour. The television station therefore needs to find out about its viewers on a regular basis. A *longitudinal* research design gathers information on a number of occasions over time. The television station might ask viewers on a regular basis to tell the researcher what they have watched in order to help the station's owners and programme makers track any changes in the public's television viewing.

Longitudinal, or *continuous, research* depends on talking to the same people, or same types of people, on different occasions over a long period. To help achieve this, many organizations set up *panels* or groups of respondents, who agree to participate regularly in the research project. In this way, the television station's researchers could be sure that any changes they identified really were changes in their viewers' viewing patterns, rather than the result of asking about the behaviour of a different group of people.

Ad hoc or continuous? Practice task

Look again at the research problems in the practice task on page 24. In each case, decide whether the research problem requires cross-sectional or longitudinal research. Check your answers on page 139.

Creating the right research design

As we have seen, choosing a research design depends on knowing whether you need:

▧ primary or secondary research;

▧ qualitative or quantitative information;

▧ exploratory, descriptive or causal research;

▧ a cross-sectional study or a longitudinal study.

It is important to recognize, however, that many research problems require not just one type of research. It may be necessary to plan different phases, using different approaches. In this way, each phase can inform the next. It is not unusual, for example, for a project to combine an initial, qualitative exploratory phase with a later quantitative descriptive phase. These two phases could be combined into one ad hoc project, with different information being investigated in each phase.

Research designs in practice

Earlier, we looked at the problems facing the owners of a newspaper who needed to decide if they should change the size and look of the paper. The owners need an ad hoc project, because they need to gather the information to make the decision soon. However, they have no idea how their readers would react to the planned changes – or if they would gain new readers. Table 3.1 outlines two possible approaches they could take.

Table 3.1   *Two possible research approaches*

Approach 1	Approach 2
Phase 1	Phase 1
Descriptive: An initial quantitative phase, gathering information about how a large number of readers view the paper in its current form. *This would help the owners see what their readers really like and dislike.*	*Exploratory: An initial qualitative phase, exploring the reactions of a small group of readers to the proposed changes.* *This would help identify a range of possible reactions to the planned changes.*
Phase 2	Phase 2
Exploratory: A follow-up qualitative study could use the information from Phase 1 to identify what changes the readers might like, then test these out with a group representing the readers.	*Descriptive: A follow-up quantitative study could use the information from Phase 1 to identify the changes that are likely to be most popular then find out if these are liked by a larger group of readers.*

As the example shows, there may be a number of different ways to research the problem. Each has its own strengths. Approach 1 could be useful if the newspaper owners are very unsure about the types of changes to make and they need to know what their readers really like. Approach 2, however, is more appropriate if the owners have a clear idea of the changes needed, and need to gauge how popular they will be. Before making the final choice of design, therefore, the researcher needs to ask a series of questions:

■   **What is already known?** Recheck the background to the problem, and check this if possible with the client. The client might have some information – from discussion with colleagues or through knowledge of a rival newspaper – that did not appear in the background section of the brief.

■ **What has already been decided?** The newspaper owners might know exactly what kind of changes they want to make, and further research into other options might not change their minds. The researcher needs to know what is non-negotiable.

■ **What really needs to be decided?** It is important to gain a real understanding of the decision that has to be made. In the case of the newspaper, is it, 'We want to make these changes. What will the impact be?' or is it, 'We want to make changes. Which ones should we make?' Having a real understanding of the business problem will help guide the researcher to the best design.

■ **When is the information needed, and how much money is available for the project?** It's vital to realize that, with most projects, the researcher needs to understand business practicalities. It's no good designing the perfect project, but ignoring the fact that it will take too long and cost too much. The research design you choose will only be the right design if it can be completed within the budget and time allocated by the client.

As we saw in Chapter 2, these are questions which might be answered in the brief. However, the researcher must recheck these before beginning to put together a proposal for the project.

Beginning the research proposal

The research proposal forms the basis of the research project. It can serve many functions, such as:

■ **A competitive document.** Many clients will ask a number of research agencies to compete for the same project, and select the proposal that most closely meets their requirements.

■ A **binding contract.** The proposal tells the client what the researcher plans to do, and how much it will cost. If the client is commissioning an outside agency to carry out the research, the proposal may form the basis of the contract between the client and the supplier.

■ **A working plan.** In some cases, the client and the researcher may use the proposal to provide a basis for the project plan, identifying key dates for the completion of different stages. If it is used as a plan for the project, the client and the researcher may also revisit it at different stages to see if they wish to amend what was initially planned.

A well-written proposal should demonstrate that the researcher fully understands the client's business problem, and how the planned research will address that problem. As we saw earlier, the proposed research design may be constrained by limits set by the client. However, in the proposal, researchers need to show how they have worked within these constraints to design the most appropriate research solution within the time and financial budgets.

Drafting the proposal

The amount of detail contained in the proposal will depend on the client's needs and on the project itself. However, all proposals should include the following sections:

▓ **Background.** The proposal should show that the researcher has really understood the business problem. This section allows researchers to discuss the problem in their own words, and identify key issues for the client's business or organization.

▓ **Research design.** A clear description is needed of the chosen design, along with some justification for its use. If there are any limitations to the design, the researcher needs to say how these will be addressed. For example, there may not be time to meet all of the client's requirements or with the budget available, so the researcher needs to show how any issues not met in this project might be addressed later.

▓ **Methods.** How is the researcher going to collect and analyse the information? In Section 2 of this book, we look at what needs to be included here.

▓ **'Deliverables'.** What will the client get for their money? How will the researcher ensure that the information provided is the most useful for the client? For more information on the details to include in this section, see Chapter 8

▓ **Timing and cost.** The client will expect to see a detailed plan of when the different stages of the project will be completed, and how much the different elements will cost.

▓ **Personnel.** Who is going to work on the project? This section should demonstrate why the different team members are the best people to undertake the research.

Creating a research design: case study

The owners of T H Stores have decided to commission research into the advisability of enlarging their current supermarket. They could convert part of the warehouse space in their current store into more retail space, and they have planning permission to do this. However, they need to be sure that the extension would be worth the extra investment.

Go back to Chapter 2 and re-read the information given on pages 15 to 17 about T H Stores, then review the 'quantitative or qualitative' task on page 22. What type of research design would you recommend for this project? Note down your recommendations, including reasons for your choices. Then compare your answer with the suggestion on page 139. Don't forget that there is no 'correct' design. However, it is vital to know why a research design is appropriate – or not.

Terminology test

The following research terms were introduced in this chapter. Can you explain what each one means?

- research design
- secondary research
- qualitative research
- exploratory research
- causal research
- cross-sectional research
- continuous research

- primary research
- quantitative research
- panels
- descriptive research
- ad hoc research
- longitudinal research

Summary

A good understanding of the client's needs and the research objectives will help you choose the best research design. Don't forget to:

- Find out what exists already. Good secondary research can save time and money.

- Decide whether the client needs information that provides strong, statistical evidence or gives a more in-depth analysis of what people are thinking.

- Assess whether the research needs to explore a new area, get reactions to a new idea, describe the situation as it is, or find links between different aspects of the same problem.

- Think about time – are you taking a 'snapshot' or trying to find out if an issue changes over time?

- Plan within your budget. An effective research design always takes consideration of the time and money the client has available.

In this chapter, we have looked at the first stage in creating a research project – choosing the best design. All of the other methods included in the proposal depend on the design being the most appropriate for the client and the business problem.

How can I gather the information?

Identifying different research methods

Introduction

Once the overall design of a research project has been selected, it is important to identify exactly how you are going to gather the information, and how you are going to ensure that it is accurate.

In this chapter, you will learn how to:

- select appropriate sources of secondary ***data***;
- consider whether the secondary data you are gathering is useful;
- identify and describe a range of options for gathering primary data;
- choose appropriate methods of data collection for different types of research problems.

Dealing with data

In previous chapters, we referred to researchers as gatherers and analysts of 'information'. However, a more accurate term for the material they gather is 'data'. 'Datum' is an individual piece of information, and the plural 'data' refers only to numerous pieces of information.

Therefore, in specialist and scientific texts, you may find statements such as 'The data are incomplete.' However, in everyday use, the word data is more often used to mean one or more pieces of information, and you are more likely to hear 'The data is incomplete.' In this book, we have used the word in this everyday sense.

Gathering secondary data

Secondary data has a key role to play in research projects. By gathering existing information from different sources and reviewing it in line with the research objectives, the researcher can save time and money. In some cases, it may be possible to address the objectives using secondary data alone.

However, secondary data should be treated with caution. It must be remembered that the information was collected not for the purposes of your research project, but for other reasons. For example, customer reactions to a product may have been collected to help market that product. If you are researching the strengths and weaknesses of the product, you need to remember that negative reactions may not have been included.

To make sure that secondary data really is useful for your project, therefore, it is important to ask the following questions about each data source and each set of data:

■ **Who produced the data – and why?** This is a particularly vital question to ask when searching the internet for secondary data. Good research depends on having data which is accurate and unbiased. However, research reports may be produced by individuals or organizations that have an interest in promoting a particular view. For example, an organization that produces armaments may wish to minimize possible criticism of the danger to civilians of its products, while a political pressure group may wish to highlight this danger. Reports and articles found on the internet may be published by either group, possibly presenting a biased account of the situation. Knowing who produced the information – and why it was published – will help you evaluate how useful the data is to your own research project.

■ **Whose opinions and reactions are described in the data?** Articles and research reports might not present the views of the people or organization who commissioned them, but they might still be biased. It is important to know whose opinions were sought in previous research so that you can judge how useful the information is to your project. For example, if a food company is seeking ways to improve the packaging of its products, it needs to find out the views of all those who currently use the product. If previous research only presents the views of satisfied customers, the researcher should ensure that the current project also finds out about those who were not satisfied. You might also need to consider where the research was carried out. For example, many university projects are carried out amongst students. This means that the results are likely to represent mostly younger people and will not be representative of the wider population.

As well as knowing who contributed to previous research, it's also necessary to know how many people were contacted. For example, the usefulness of a quantitative research report might be limited if only a small number of people contributed their views.

■ **How old is the data?** Finding out the dates of reports, articles or other information is vital to help researchers decide how relevant the data is to their project. A clear example of this can be seen when we consider the use of sales records as secondary data. If the food company mentioned above wants to find out if its new packaging is affecting sales levels, it needs to examine its sales records from before and after the point when changes were made. Using sales records from an earlier period will not provide an appropriate comparison.

■ **How comprehensive is the data?** As we saw in Chapter 3, the client may be able to provide a lot of secondary data from the company's records. However, the researcher needs to check how complete the records are. A company that needs to build a profile of its range of customers may use sales and marketing records to do this. These records may provide information about each customer's age, address, profession and so on. However, if some of the records omit some of this necessary information, the researcher will have more difficulty drawing up the profile. It is therefore vital that the researcher checks how complete the records are in general before identifying the areas that can be included in the profile.

■ **How accessible is the data?** In addition to questions about the accuracy and range of secondary data, the researcher needs to find out if it is stored in an accessible format. This can create particular problems if records are stored electronically, in formats that the client no longer uses.

In addition to technological considerations preventing access to data, the researcher may also face ethical issues in using secondary data. In many countries, data protection legislation means that there are very clear rules governing how information about individuals may and may not be used. Furthermore, other issues such as copyright may mean that researchers cannot use the data in the way they wish. In the UK, the MRS Code of Conduct provides clear guidance on how data may, and may not, be used. Wherever they are working, researchers need to make sure that they are aware of any restrictions on the use of the data which they find.

Although a phase of secondary research in a research project can save time and costs, care needs to be taken to ensure that the data which the researcher finds is really useful and relevant. Use the checklist in the box to help you evaluate the usefulness of the data you find.

Secondary data sources: Selection checklist

■ **Check the name of the author and publisher of any report or article.** If you have never heard of them before, do a web search to find out as much as you can about them. How reliable do you think they are as a source?

■ **Check the date of publication.** If the report or article is more than five years old, search the web for more up-to-date literature with a similar title.

■ **Look at the details of who the respondents were in any previous research – and how many people responded.** Section 2 of this book will help you evaluate whether a project has included an appropriate number and range of respondents.

■ **Speak to the people responsible for creating and keeping records.** If you intend to use the client's records, try to find out how comprehensive they are before deciding what categories of information you will take from them.

■ **Check IT formats and requirements.** Have you got the appropriate technology? Check on what is needed to read records and reports before you begin the research process.

■ **Check – and double-check – any restrictions on the use of the data you find.** Researchers are obliged to adhere to strict ethical guidelines. Make sure you are aware of these by reading the MRS Code of Conduct. If you are outside the UK, you should also check with local market research bodies to find out about ethical restrictions which are specific to your country or region.

Secondary research makes use of data that has already been recorded in reports, journals and other types of records. However, most research projects will also need to gather information from the people and places directly affected by the research project. For example, T H Stores, which you read about in Chapters 2 and 3, can only find out about its current customers' views of its plans by asking those customers. There are many ways of gathering this primary data, and the method you choose will depend on a range of criteria.

Gathering data for primary research

As we saw in Chapter 3, primary data can be qualitative or quantitative. A range of different tools exists for gathering each type of data, and these tools can be used in different ways. In this section, we examine the most commonly used tools for collecting quantitative and qualitative data, and show how each tool can be used by the researcher.

Gathering quantitative data

Another name for quantitative research which gathers data from respondents is a *survey*. The aim of a survey is to gather data from many different respondents with the aim of measuring their responses. This might range from a national census, which measures information about the lives and habits of a country's population, to a customer service survey, which measures how happy a company's customers are with the service the company provides.

In later chapters, we shall examine in more detail how this measurement happens. However, all surveys have one thing in common: in order to ensure that they are measuring the same range of responses from all respondents, they need to be sure that all respondents are being asked the same questions. In quantitative research, a well-written questionnaire is vital.

A questionnaire

A questionnaire contains a range of **structured questions**, each with a set of possible responses. The questions are 'structured', meaning that the wording is precise and will not change, even if an interviewer is putting the question to 50 different respondents. Respondents most often choose their answer to a question from a range of set options. Structured questionnaires can include questions recording the respondent's own words using **open-ended questions** but analysing all the different answers is time-consuming and these types of questions are therefore kept to a minimum. By tightly controlling both the questions and the possible answers, the researcher can measure the respondents' responses.

For more information on designing an effective structured questionnaire, see Chapter 8.

Collecting data using a questionnaire

The questionnaire is the main tool used in quantitative research. It can be completed by the respondents themselves (a self-completion questionnaire) or it can be completed by an interviewer who asks the respondent the questions and records the answers (an interviewer-administered questionnaire).

Self-completion questionnaires
Self-completion questionnaires rely on individual respondents to complete and return the questionnaires to the researcher or company. Self-completion questionnaires have a number of advantages. They can be sent to large numbers of potential respondents, and the cost of administering the questionnaire is relatively low because there are no interviewers involved. However, because self-completion depends entirely on the willingness

of individuals both to fill out the questionnaire and return it to the researcher, response rates can be very low. The level of response will often depend on how long the questionnaire is and how much time the respondent has to spend on it. Response is also affected by the level of interest the respondent has in the topic. Response rates can be very high when asking sports fans about sport, but would probably be much lower if the same group was asked about washing powder. Companies may try to encourage greater response by offering incentives such as the chance to enter a prize draw if recipients return a completed questionnaire.

Self-completion questionnaires can be sent and returned in a variety of different ways. Each way has its own benefits and drawbacks for the researcher:

Collecting data using self-completion questionnaires

These are some of the most common methods of collecting data using a self-completion questionnaire:

■ **Postal surveys.** Respondents can post their questionnaires back to the researcher.
  ✔ This can be a fairly inexpensive way of gathering data as postage costs are low.
  ✘ Time is required to allow as many respondents as possible to complete and return the questionnaire. The inconvenience involved in having to post the questionnaire can lead to low response rates.

■ **Internet surveys.** Respondents can complete an online questionnaire, where questions only appear when the previous question has been answered. Respondents are directed to a website where they can complete the questionnaire. To direct respondents to the website hosting the questionnaire you need to know their e-mail address and have permission to e-mail them, or use a pop-up on another website to invite them. Many research companies maintain panels of people who have agreed to complete questionnaires online.
  ✔ The data feeds directly into the researcher's computer program, which makes analysis easier.
  ✘ Not all potential respondents necessarily have access to the internet.

■ **E-mail surveys.** Questionnaires may be attached to e-mails, and respondents complete and return via e-mail. Again, you need to know the e-mail address of the respondents and have their permission to e-mail them.
  ✔ This can be quicker and more effective than postal surveys at reaching a wide audience.
  ✘ If respondents want to remain anonymous, they may not want to return a questionnaire from their own e-mail address.
  ✘ It can be inconvenient for the respondent to open an attachment, save it, complete it and then attach it to a return e-mail. This can lead to low response rates.

■ **Self-completion satisfaction questionnaires.** Have you ever completed a questionnaire in a restaurant, hotel or shop? These questionnaires are often used to measure customer satisfaction.
  ✔ The researchers can be sure of reaching the people they want to question.
  ✘ They might get most responses from customers who are dissatisfied with the service and want to complain.

Interviewer-administered interviews

These interviews rely on an interviewer to 'deliver' the questionnaire – to ask the questions precisely as they are worded, and to record the answers. A variety of different ways exist both for asking the questions and recording responses.

Collecting data using interviews

These are some of the most common methods of collecting data using interviewer-administered interviews:

- **Face-to-face interviews.** These are carried out by interviewers approaching potential respondents, often in the street or going door-to-door. Responses are recorded on paper copies of the questionnaire.
  - ✔ A personal approach may encourage people to participate as respondents.
  - ✘ Interviews need to take place at a time when interviewers are likely to meet the range of people who need to be interviewed. For example, if they want to find out what residents in a particular street think about council proposals for parking in the area, the interviewers probably need to go in the evening, when most people are at home.

- **CAPI (computer-assisted personal interviewing).** This is a variant on traditional face-to-face interviewing, carried out by interviewers who read the questionnaire and record responses using a hand-held computer or a lap-top.
  - ✔ The computer displays only one question at a time. This avoids the potential for the interviewer to miss or skip questions, as can happen when questionnaires are completed with paper and pen.
  - ✔ Entering responses directly into a computer allows the data to be analysed more quickly and easily.
  - ✔ It is more difficult for interviewer to make a mistake and ask the wrong question as which question to ask is programmed into the computer.
  - ✘ It is expensive to provide all the interviewers with a computer and to train them in using the technology.

- **Telephone interviews.** Many interviews are carried out by interviewers over the phone. Like traditional face-to-face interviewers, telephone interviewers may complete the questionnaire with pen and paper.
  - ✔ Interviewers working from a central location – usually a call centre – can contact potential respondents in a wide geographical area.
  - ✘ People may be unwilling to answer questions asked by someone they have not met. The skilled telephone interviewer needs to engage the respondent at a very early stage in the conversation.
  - ✘ It is not possible to show pictures or other materials. As a result, evaluating new ideas using this approach can be difficult.

- **CATI (computer-assisted telephone interviewing).** This is a variant on telephone interviewing, with interviewers reading the questionnaire and recording answers using specialized computer equipment.

✔ CATI equipment allows the quality of interviewing and the recording of responses to be monitored by the organization.

✔ Data can be fed directly into an electronic analysis software package, so it can be processed and analysed very quickly

✘ CATI equipment can be expensive. This type of interviewing is normally carried out by specialized companies or departments.

Data collection: methods check

Look at these descriptions of data collection in action. In each case, identify the method of data collection being used.

1. A train company wants to know what its customers think of its service. Two people have been hired to hand out questionnaires and return envelopes on selected trains.

2. In a busy exhibition centre, two representatives of an advertising company stop passers-by and ask them their views on the products available at the exhibition. The answers are entered into a small computer.

3. At work, you receive an e-mailed invitation to participate in a survey into the type of music you like to listen to. All you need to do is to click on a web link, listen to some music extracts and complete the questions that appear on the screen.

4. A major supermarket chain wants to find out what customers think of the layout of its stores. As the majority of customers have given their contact details when they signed up for loyalty cards, they can be contacted by phone. The interviewer uses a computer screen to read the questions and record responses.

Compare your answers with those on page 140.

Letting technology talk

Although the questionnaire is the tool most people associate with gathering quantitative data, recent developments in technology have allowed researchers to gather information about products and consumers in new ways.

Some technologies track the movement of goods. When an item in a supermarket or other shop is scanned through the till, electronic point-of-sale (EPOS) technology records what has been bought and when. These records help retailers to identify easily what items are the most popular, and to audit sales.

This type of technology can also help retailers understand the habits and preferences of their individual customers. Store loyalty cards, which customers present at the till when paying for their purchases, identify individual shoppers, and EPOS identifies what they bought when they used the card. In this way, the retailer can target its marketing to the individual, offering special offers and discounts on the items that particular person is likely to buy. The retailer can also see which products tend to be bought at the same time, and can use this to help position things in store to make them easier to find.

Technology is also allowing the goods to 'talk'. Recent developments have enabled manufacturers to use tiny transmitters, called radio frequency identifier tags (RFIDs), contained in a product's packaging, to track a product's movements from manufacturer to consumer.

These technological developments can also be used to involve consumers themselves in collecting data for research. For example, a research company that wants to collect data on consumer buying habits may equip a panel of respondents with barcode scanners in their homes. The respondents scan everything they buy, and the data is transmitted back to the research company. Technology-equipped panels are also used to gather data on television viewing. In these projects, electronic viewing meters are installed in the respondents' homes. The meters measure which channels are watched, and for how long. In this way, it is possible to measure national viewing figures for different channels and programmes.

These examples demonstrate how technology is providing new and sophisticated approaches to gathering data that allow companies to measure the flow of goods and the response of consumers. However, in many cases, it may be important to gain a deeper understanding of why people make the choices which they do. In these cases, a more qualitative approach is required.

Gathering qualitative data

Unlike methods used to collect quantitative data, qualitative methods usually aim to encourage respondents to talk in depth about their opinions, feelings or reactions. However, it must be remembered that, just as in quantitative research, the aim of qualitative research is to gather data that is relevant to the research objectives.

The main tool the qualitative researcher needs when collecting data is a *topic guide* (sometimes called an *interview guide*). The topic guide usually takes the form of a list of questions, prompts or topic areas which respondents are asked to talk about. Unlike a structured questionnaire, the questions in a topic guide are always open-ended, requiring respondents to give an extended answer in their own words.

Topic guides are the key tool for those carrying out qualitative interviews with individuals (*depth interviews*) or with groups of people (*discussion groups*, also known as *focus groups*).

Depth (or in-depth) interviews are carried out by specially trained interviewers and are used for a wide variety of reasons.

Collecting data using depth interviews: key features

Where?
■ Depth interviews can be carried out face-to-face, often in the respondent's home or workplace. They can also be carried out by telephone, although this does not allow the interviewer the opportunity to observe how the respondent reacts when questions are asked.

Who's involved?
■ The role of the depth interviewer is to draw as much information as possible from the respondent, while ensuring that the information is relevant to the research objectives. Unlike interviewers using structured questionnaires, depth interviewers create their own questions using the topic guide for guidance.

How is the interview handled?
■ The topic guide provides the framework for the interview, ensuring that all necessary areas are covered. In projects where a number of different interviewers are employed, it is vital that they review the topic guide together to ensure they are all giving the necessary areas enough attention.

How is data recorded?
■ It is vital to record the information the respondent provides. In addition to taking notes, the interviewer usually makes an audio or video recording of the interview.

Why use depth interviews?
■ Depth interviews are extremely useful in studies into sensitive subjects, where respondents might be unlikely to express their views in front of others. The setting of the interview and the creation of rapport between the interviewer and respondent are important in these cases, so that the respondents feel confident and comfortable in sharing their views.
■ Depths are also used frequently in business-to-business research, where it may be difficult to research the views of busy senior managers.

Variations
■ Variants on the individual depth interview include **duos** or **trios**, where the interviewer interviews groups of two or three respondents from the same family, the same group of friends or the same company. This approach can be useful in exploring areas that normally involve group decisions, such as research into family television viewing habits. By speaking to the family members together, the interviewer can gain insight into the way the individuals interact when deciding which television programmes to watch.

Like duos and trios, discussion groups can provide insight into the ways people interact with each other. They also provide opportunities for individual respondents to spark reactions in each other, resulting in lots of new ideas.

Collecting data using discussion groups: key features

Where?

■ Discussion groups are usually held in central locations, such as interviewers' homes. However, purpose-built **viewing facilities** are also used. These are rooms equipped with audio and/or video recording equipment and two-way mirrors, allowing the researcher or the client to observe the group in action without disturbing the discussion.

Who's involved?

■ Respondents for discussion groups are usually identified by a **recruiter**. Like the interviewers who collect quantitative data, recruiters need to find individuals who are willing to participate as respondents. However, recruiters have no role in collecting data. Their role is to create groups of respondents – with usually around eight respondents per group – and ensure that they are briefed about the aims of the project and the location of the group.

■ The discussion group is conducted by the **moderator**, whose role is to ensure that everyone contributes and that the discussion is kept on track.

How is the discussion group conducted?

■ Using the topic guide, the moderator's task is to ensure that discussion between respondents is generated around the key research areas. Different tasks might be used to generate different types of information. For example, a company wishing to develop a name for a new chocolate bar might use discussion groups to identify how consumers 'see' the product. The moderator might ask respondents to draw what they think of when they taste the chocolate, or think of five adjectives to describe the taste. Moderating can be difficult if there are dominant individuals in the group, or if the respondents don't get along with each other, but, like an orchestra conductor, a skilled moderator can guide the participants to work together successfully.

How is the data recorded?

■ Discussion groups are usually recorded on video, to allow the researcher both to listen to the discussion and observe the interaction between the respondents.

Why use discussion groups?

■ Well-run discussion groups can generate a lot of information in a very short time. They are particularly useful for projects that need to produce new ideas or solve problems, since, when the group works together, it can come up with a wide range of solutions.

Variations

■ One variation on the group is the mini-group. These are particularly useful for research into very specialized areas, such as science or health specialisms. It is often difficult to recruit larger groups with enough expert knowledge to contribute ideas, so mini-groups of three or four specialists may be held.

Watch what's happening: collecting data through observation

Discussion groups are often video recorded to allow researchers to see as well as listen to the interaction between respondents. This type of observation can provide useful data, as the researcher can analyse how respondents react physically to different ideas and materials. For example, if respondents are asked to taste the chocolate bar that needs new packaging, their expressions and gestures may show what they think. Analysing this type of body language is an important part of qualitative research, and some techniques depend entirely on watching rather than talking to respondents.

Observation techniques are important for a wide range of studies, and can be used to collect either quantitative or qualitative data. For example, if a supermarket wants to know how best to lay out its different departments, researchers may watch customers as they move through the store, tracking the routes they take. This is using observation for quantitative purposes – measuring and analysing the customers' journeys can identify areas of the store which are least visited, and help the owners make better use of the space. A qualitative analysis of the same journey might try to identify why the customers took the routes they chose. This type of analysis tries to work out individuals' motivations for their actions rather than simply describe what they do.

One popular method for collecting both quantitative and qualitative is *mystery shopping*. Mystery shopping is often used by businesses to find out how their staff respond to customers. Using this method, the researcher, disguised as a shopper, will undertake a range of shopping 'tasks'. These might range from buying an item to making a serious complaint about the business's products or services. Once the shopping tasks are complete, the mystery shopper makes notes on what has happened. These might record quantitative information (such as how long the assistant took to complete the sale) or qualitative data (for example, describing the assistant's reactions to an awkward customer).

Although mystery shopping is regarded as an observation technique, it need not involve the researcher watching the staff member. The mystery customer might carry out the shopping task by phone, and record the outcomes in the same way.

Methods matching: revision task

Look at the data collection methods in the left-hand column of Table 4.1, and match each with its description in the right-hand column. Compare your answers with those on page 140.

Table 4.1 *Methods matching*

1. CATI	A) electronic recording of purchases, at the time of purchase
2. Mini-groups	B) face-to-face interview, using a questionnaire, where interviewer records responses on a hand-held computer
3. Topic guide	C) interviews carried out by phone, with responses fed directly into a computer
4. Duo	D) moderated discussions often used in specialist areas, where there is a limited number of specialists
5. EPOS	E) observation method often used for research into an organization's customer service
6. Mystery shopping	F) qualitative interview with two people together
7. CAPI	G) a list of areas or prompts which helps moderators and qualitative interviewers ensure all necessary areas are covered

Choosing the best research method

There are many factors involved in choosing the best research method for your project. In Section 2 we shall look at these in more detail, but here is a useful checklist to consider:

■ **What kind of information do you need?** Qualitative or quantitative? Or both? This will help you identify the types of methods you can use.

■ **What resources do you have access to?** This includes both technology and human resources. If the organization does not already have the IT necessary for the computer-assisted methods, it may be too expensive to invest in them. However, there are companies that provide data collection services, so you may be able to brief them about the project.

■ **How are you going to select the people you need to interview?** You need to identify precisely the different groups of people whose opinions matter to the research project. We shall look at how to do this in Chapter 5.

■ **How are you going to analyse the data once it has been collected?** Forward planning is essential when choosing a data collection method. If you distribute 1,000 postal questionnaires, you need to remember that someone has to record and collate all of the information on the returned questionnaires. Time and resources for dealing with data need to be built in to your research plan from the beginning.

In this chapter, we have looked at a range of different methods for collecting research data. As with all stages in the research process, your choice will be governed by the research aims and the time and resources you have available.

Collecting data: case study

The owners of T H Stores have commissioned a research consultant to carry out research into the advisability of enlarging their store. The consultant has decided that they need to find out what existing customers would like to see in a larger store, and what features would attract new customers to the store. The owners realize that good data collection is vital to a successful research project and are willing to hire a data collection company to support the consultant if he or she feels this is necessary.

What data collection method or methods would you recommend for this project? Make notes about your recommendations, including reasons for your choices.

Compare your answer with the suggestions on pages 140–41. Remember that a number of different approaches might be suitable – each has its own strengths and limitations.

Terminology test

The following research terms were introduced in this chapter. Can you explain what each one means?

- data
- questionnaire
- topic guide
- depth interview
- trio
- focus group
- recruiter
- observation
- CAPI
- EPOS

- survey
- structured questions
- open-ended questions
- duo
- discussion group
- viewing facilities
- moderator
- mystery shopping
- CATI
- RFID

Summary

Selecting the most appropriate data collection method can be a complex task. Remember:

■ The method you choose will depend on the type of information you need. Don't be afraid to use both quantitative and qualitative techniques in the same project.

■ Your choice of method will be constrained by the time and money you have available. Remember – the more respondents you need, the more expensive and time-consuming it will be to collect the data.

■ There might be a number of different techniques that could be used to collect data for your project. Try to think of the strengths and limitations of each one before you make your choice.

■ At the beginning of a project, it's easy to forget that all data that is collected needs to be processed: it needs to be checked, collated and analysed. Don't just select a method of data collection – plan your approach to analysis at the same time.

Designing a research project: the tools of market research

Who should I talk to?

Understanding how sampling works

Introduction

Before beginning to collect data for a research project, the researcher needs to know exactly who to include in the research. Planning who to gather data from, how many respondents are needed, and how to contact respondents is all part of the sampling plan.

In this chapter, you will learn how to:

■ define what is meant by a research **sample**;

■ identify the ***population of interest*** for a project;

■ identify and describe a range of sampling methods;

■ describe the elements required in a ***sampling plan*** for a research project.

What is a 'research sample'?

Primary research depends on gathering data from different respondents. However, before beginning the process of collecting data, the researcher needs to identify exactly who should be asked to provide data. It is usually impossible to interview everyone who has an interest in the project. Therefore, the researcher needs to identify a *sample*: a selection of people who can be seen as representative of all of the different groups of people who might be affected by, or have an interest in, the subject being researched. These groups together are known as the *population of interest*.

The aim of sampling is to gather data that can be seen as representative of the views of the population of interest as a whole. This is particularly important with quantitative research, where the aim of a project is to produce data which is *valid* and *reliable*.

Validity and reliability

Valid data: Can the results from the research be generalized to the population as a whole? This is an important question, particularly in quantitative research projects. If samples and questionnaires are well devised, the researcher can be confident that the results are representative of the whole population of interest, or, in other words, that the data has validity.

Reliable data: Will I get the same results if I ask different people or if different interviewers deliver the questionnaire? The aim of quantitative research is to be sure that the data is as reliable as possible: that you will achieve similar results if you repeat the data collection, as long as the conditions of the data collection are the same. This is particularly important when teams of interviewers are working on the same project. If they are all interviewing similar groups of people, we should expect them to find similar results.

Ideally, a sample will:

■ Contain representatives from all of the different groups affected by the research. It is important that a sample reflects the entire population of interest.

■ Balance the number of respondents from each group within the population of interest. For example, a car manufacturer knows that 60 per cent of the buyers of a particular model of car are men under the age of 30. It wants to launch a new model in the same market. The sample therefore should contain an appropriate proportion of men in this age group. The representation of different groups in the sample should usually be in proportion to the groups' representation in the population of interest.

■ Contain enough members for the information that is gathered to be generalizable to the population as a whole.

Identifying an appropriate sample

There are a number of important steps involved in identifying an appropriate sample for your research project.

Step 1: Identify the population of interest

The population of interest might include a number of different groups. In Chapter 3, you read about the owners of a newspaper who want to change the size and layout of their paper. For this project, it is important to find out about the views of their current readers. However, there are other groups whose opinions might be very important. These other groups might include potential new readers or purchasers and other stakeholders, such as the newspaper's clients, as the following examples show:

■ The newspaper owners want to increase the circulation of their paper: in other words, they want new readers. It's therefore important to find out about the views of people who don't currently read their newspaper, but who might read a similar newspaper, to find out if the changes would encourage them to change their choice of paper.

■ Newspapers depend on advertisers for a large proportion of their income. Finding out what advertisers think of the changes may have an important impact on the changes which can be made.

It's important to make sure that the sample includes representatives from all of the groups in the population of interest.

Step 2: Think about how many people you need to speak to

The number of people included in your sample will depend on three important considerations:

■ **Are you doing quantitative research or qualitative research?** The aim of quantitative research is to provide confident measurements of what people think. To be confident that your data is valid and reliable, you need to gather data from a large sample of your population of interest. However, qualitative research usually depends on much smaller samples. This is because the aim of the project is usually to uncover a range of ideas on a subject, rather than measure how widely held they are.

■ **How easy is it to contact your sample?** In some areas of research it can be very difficult to create a large sample simply because the people you would like to speak to are very difficult to contact. This can be the case when you need to interview senior managers, specialists, or even people who simply don't have a phone.

■ **How much time and money do you have?** Gathering data requires time and resources – and the more respondents there are, the more time and resources you need. When planning the sample size, it's important to recognize what is 'do-able' within your resources.

In quantitative research, it is generally assumed that larger samples will produce more reliable data. However, it is important to be practical: setting the size of the sample will always require a balance between a larger number of respondents and keeping the project affordable.

Step 3: Identify who is in your sample – and where they are

An effective sample depends on knowing where and how to find respondents. In some cases, this might be quite simple. For example, a company that wants to carry out a customer satisfaction survey might already have a list of all its customers. The researcher can use this list to identify an appropriate number and range of customers to invite to become respondents. The list of customers is used as the *sample frame*, the list of all members of the population of interest from which the sample is drawn.

However, many research projects are carried out without a sample frame. For example, interviewers carrying out interviews in a supermarket may approach potential respondents because they fall into a target age group or family grouping. Interviewers in these situations will often have quotas to fulfil. For example, they might need to interview 20 women aged 25 to 34, and 15 men aged 35 to 44, in order to reflect the make-up of the population interest.

If a project depends on a quota approach to sampling, the interviewers must be sure they are interviewing in the best place at the best time in order to fulfil the quota. For example, an interviewer in a supermarket on a weekday morning might be able to interview large numbers of retired people, but would be unlikely to find many people in full-time work.

Identifying the population of interest: practice task

Look at the following research projects. For each one, identify the group or groups of people who should be included in the population of interest.

1. A company that sells clothes by mail order wants to find out how satisfied its customers are with its range of products.

2. Six months ago, a local council launched a scheme to encourage residents in its area to recycle more. It now wants to measure how successful this has been.

3. A manufacturer of luxury ice cream is planning to launch a range of new flavours, for sale in its own chain of cafés and ice-cream shops.

Compare your answers with those on page 141.

Choosing the right sampling method

Some research projects aim to gather data from all of the people in the population of interest. This approach, which can be used in both qualitative and quantitative studies, is known as a *census*.

The national census

In many countries, a national census is carried out every few years by the government to find out how the lives of citizens are changing. The national census is a huge quantitative project, which aims to gather data about everyone in the country at the time of the census. The results can be used by the government, business and local communities to help plan future developments.

In the UK, the national census takes place every 10 years, and the data collected during a census can be accessed by everyone online. To find out more about the UK census, and to view some of the data, go to www.statistics.gov.uk/census

A census allows the researcher to gather information from everyone in the population of interest. As a result, it can provide a guarantee of valid data. However, a census has two major drawbacks: it is very expensive to run, and in most cases it is not possible to contact everyone in the population of interest. Therefore, when planning a research project, it is important to consider how you are going to select respondents.

Selecting a sampling approach for quantitative research

It is important to remember that the aim of quantitative research is to provide valid, reliable data on which decisions can be based. Therefore, it's vital that the researcher chooses a sample that is likely to reflect the views and behaviours of the population of interest as a whole.

Sampling in quantitative research is approached in two main ways: *random sampling* (also known as *probability sampling*) and *non-random sampling* (also known as *non-probability sampling*). In this section, we shall look at each approach in turn.

Random sampling: key features
The most important feature of random sampling is that everyone in the population of interest has an equal chance of being selected as a respondent. This selection can be done in a number of different ways, depending on how the population of interest is structured, and the research that needs to be done. Think about the local council that wants to measure the success of its recycling scheme. It probably has a list of all the households in its area that are covered by the scheme, which it can use as a sample frame. There are

2,100 households in the area, and the council has decided to gather data from 300. The box demonstrates how a range of different approaches to random sampling might be applied to this example.

Creating a random sample for the recycling scheme

■ **Simple random sampling.** With simple random sampling you allocate each household a number from 1 to 2,100 and then, using a program that generates random numbers or random number tables, select 300 numbers at random. These are the households you want to interview. There is a good chance, however, that this 300 will not be spread evenly across the list of 2,100. For example, you might find that 150 households in the sample are drawn from the first 200 in the population. This means that simple random sampling may give a sample that is concentrated in certain streets. These streets would be over-represented in the sample, while other streets would be under-represented.

■ **Interval sampling.** In the example, it is important that the sample is spread evenly across the population of interest so that all streets are represented. Therefore, it is best to use interval sampling. In this approach, you first need to divide the number in the population (2,100) by the number you want in the sample (300). The answer, 7, indicates that you should choose every seventh household as for the sample. This is the *sampling interval.* The next step is to give a number to each household, and to start counting from a random start point, generated by a random number program or taken from a table of random numbers. If our random start point is 5, we should choose every seventh household from number 5 onwards to be in the sample. In this way, each household has the same probability of being chosen and the sample is spread evenly across the research population.

■ **Stratified random sampling.** Interval sampling ensures that the sample is spread evenly across all streets. However, if the scheme includes the collection of recyclable waste from some streets in the area but not others, the council needs to be sure that the opinions of both groups are heard. It could therefore divide the population into households that have collections and those that do not, and sample from each separately.

The council wants to collect data equally from both types of households. Therefore, it should sample each group in proportion to its place in the population as a whole:
– Group 1: Households with collections: 700 households, representing one-third of the households, so 100 are required for the sample.
– Group 2: Households without collections: 1,400 households, representing two-thirds of the households, so 200 are required for the sample.

This approach is known as *proportionate stratified random sampling.* However, there might be other differences between the households that the council knows about. For example, one street might contain small flats designed for students who only live in the area in university term time. However, the council wants to be sure that it gathers the views of the area's permanent residents. Therefore, it might decide to select fewer student households than permanent households, choosing every eighth or ninth house instead of every seventh. This approach – *disproportionate stratified random sampling* – will ensure that the permanent households have more representation in the final sample than the student households.

As the examples show, the approach to selecting a random sample will depend on how much is known about the population of interest, how it is distributed, and any weighting that needs to be given to particular groups within that population. Sometimes, for example, using either simple random sampling or interval sampling will provide a sample that it is uneconomic to interview. For example, we might want a sample of 1,000 households to be representative of all households in the UK, which has roughly 20 million households. We might also need to interview our sample face-to-face. The likelihood of selecting households that are nowhere near each other is high if we use simple random sampling, and certain if we use interval sampling. It could mean sending an interviewer to the north of Scotland for one interview and to the far south of England for another. However, there are ways to make sure that samples are both random and economically viable. *Cluster sampling* begins with identifying groups – or clusters – of areas where the sample can be drawn from, and uses a random sampling technique to select the people who should be included. *Multi-stage sampling* arrives at the sample through a series of steps, with each step reducing the number of different areas to be sampled. Again, this approach uses random sampling techniques to arrive at the final sample.

All probability, or random, sampling approaches have one thing in common: they select respondents using a mathematical formula, rather than basing selection on features of the respondents themselves. However, in many projects, using random sampling methods may not be possible for a number of reasons:

▦ **They depend on the researcher having a complete and accurate sample frame, covering all members of the population of interest.** If you don't have this, you cannot be sure that your sample is really representative of the population as a whole.

▦ **They depend on the selected respondents agreeing to participate.** As all respondents are selected before the project begins, it is important to be sure that everyone will be able to provide data. However, some people may not want to participate. If large numbers of respondents refuse to participate, the final sample could end up being very small and unrepresentative.

▦ **They depend on the interviewers being able to speak with the selected respondents.** If the data for the project is being gathered using interviews, the interviewer must speak with the selected person. However, the respondent might be out when the interviewer calls. The interviewer cannot simply interview the person in the next house. He or she must speak to the person selected by the sampling approach, and will therefore need to return when the selected respondent is at home. Having to revisit a respondent several times can significantly increase the time and money required for the data collection.

The final point is a very important one. Research projects usually need to be completed as cost-effectively as possible. Therefore, sampling methods need to be chosen which will provide an appropriate sample, but will allow the research to be completed within budget. As a result, non-probability (or non-random) sampling approaches are often used in quantitative projects.

Random sampling: methods check

There are 20 houses in Maple Street, numbered from 1 to 20. The research project needs a sample of five households from the street. Look at the examples in Figure 5.1. In each of them, the houses being sampled are identified with [tick]. Can you identify what random sampling method is being used in each case? Check your answers on page 141.

Example 1

1	3	5	7	9 ✔	11	13	15	17	19 ✔
				Maple Street					
2	4 ✔ Start here	6	8	10	12	14 ✔	16	18	20

Example 2

1	3 ✔	5 ✔	7	9	11	13	15	17	19 ✔
				Maple Street					
2	4	6	8	10	12	14 ✔	16	18	20 ✔

Example 3

Four households in the street have three or more children. These are marked in **bold**. The remaining 16 households have two or fewer children. We need one household with three or more children, and four households with two or fewer.

1 ✔	3 ✔	5	7 ✔	9	11	13	15	**17**	19
				Maple Street					
2	4	6	8	10	**12**	14 ✔	16	18 ✔	20

Figure 5.1 *Sampling Maple Street*

Non-probability sampling: key features

In non-probability sampling, respondents are chosen from the population of interest because they have certain traits or qualities. They may be chosen because of their age, their gender or some other factor. Importantly, non-probability sampling methods allow samples to be selected in projects where no complete sampling frame exists, and where there is more freedom for interviewers to select respondents.

There is a range of different approaches to non-probability sampling. We examine some of them below.

Non-probability sampling in practice

Non-probability sampling depends on the researcher identifying different groups within the population of interest. Some of the most common factors that are used to differentiate groups include the individual's:

- age;
- gender;
- marital status;
- *socio-economic group* (a description of an individual based on his or her employment status, or that of the chief income earner of his/her household, and the type of work he or she does);
- income level;
- address or home area.

When the different groups have been identified, the researcher then samples from each. This can be done in a number of ways, which are outlined in the boxes below.

Quota sampling

In this approach, the interviewer is given a quota, or number, of respondents in each of the different groups who must be interviewed. It doesn't matter who is interviewed, so long as each person meets the requirements of a particular group in the quota. However, it is important that quotas are set on relevant factors. Often, they are set by age and socio-economic group to reflect the research population. However, if the survey is about something which is used in different ways by different people, there may be additional factors in the quota. For example, if a supermarket wants to know about how consumers will react to a new convenience food, the quota may need to take into account whether there are any children in a household, and whether the parent or parents work full or part-time. These factors could have a major influence on the results. The more quotas that are set, however, the longer it will take to find people who meet the quotas.

Quota sampling is the most well-known and widely used of the non-probability approaches to sampling. Although not everyone in the population of interest has an equal chance of being a respondent, it ensures that the various different groups are represented in proportion to their presence in the population as a whole.

Random route sampling

Random route sampling is a technique that combines multi-stage probability sampling with quota sampling for sampling households. A local area, such as an electoral district, is selected using multi-stage probability sampling. Then, rather than select individual households at random from a list, a starting address is selected and the interviewer is instructed to interview at that address if possible. The interviewer is then instructed to walk in a particular direction and to interview at every 'n'th address (where n is the sampling interval). The interviewers are given instructions about turning left and right so that the route is chosen at random. The interviewers might have to continue until they complete a specified number of interviews, or alternatively they may be given quotas to fill.

Quota sampling and random route sampling can be used for large-scale and small-scale projects. However, there are several other non-probability approaches which are particularly useful when the population of interest is small or difficult to reach:

Judgement, convenience and snowball sampling

These approaches may be used when the aim of a project is to find out opinions and thoughts, rather than measure how widely held they are. As a result, they are particularly useful for finding samples for qualitative research projects. They are useful when the population of interest is quite small, but where no complete sample frame exists.

Judgement sampling

Judgement sampling is similar to quota sampling, in that researchers must identify a range of different groups within the population. However, they then use their judgement about which individuals to select, rather than depend on a quota. This is particularly useful when selecting respondents for projects investigating specialist areas. For example, a pharmaceutical company may wish to gather the views of doctors on a new drug. However, doctors are notoriously busy and not all might have prescribed the drug. In order to gather data effectively and efficiently, the researcher and client may contact a number of expert doctors whom they know are willing to give time to research projects and who have knowledge and understanding of the drug.

Convenience sampling

Convenience sampling is another method used when groups of respondents are hard to find. A convenience sample can be used when the researcher has access to a group of people who meet the criteria for the research and who are believed to be typical of the research population as a whole. The most important point about a convenience sample, however, is that the respondents can be contacted and interviewed easily. For example a manufacturer of fruit drinks wants to gauge the reaction of children to some new flavours. A local school agrees to help him and the flavours are tried out amongst several classes of the target age group. There is no reason to think that the children in this school are radically different in what they like from other children of the same age. As a result, although the sample may not be scientifically selected, it is sufficient to tell the manufacturer which flavours to pursue and which not to.

Snowball sampling

Snowball sampling enables researchers to contact hard-to-reach respondents, this time by using other respondents. For example, research into sensitive issues such as illness or political persecution may make it difficult to identify potential respondents. However, using snowball sampling, the researcher asks one respondent to put him or her in contact with another potential respondent, and so on. This technique has to be treated with care and is usually a last resort. There is a strong danger that, because they know each other, the respondents will have similar characteristics or attitudes. As a result, other groups with different characteristics and attitudes may not appear in the sample because they do not know the group that was interviewed.

All non-probability sampling approaches depend on the researcher having a clear understanding of the features of the various groups within the population of interest. Without this, it is easy to miss groups who could have an important impact on the research. Omitting key groups could lead to results which don't accurately reflect the opinions and reactions of the population of interest, and could lead the client to make the wrong business decision.

Creating a good sampling plan

As you have seen, identifying the sample to be interviewed can be complicated. However, a good sampling plan can help identify any potential problems early in the research process. Below is a list of steps which should be included in an effective sampling plan:

- **Identify precisely the population of interest.** These are all the groups of people whose views the client needs to understand in order to make the business decision.

- **Choose the sampling method(s).** The method you choose will depend on what you already know about the different groups in the population of interest. It is possible to use one method for one group of people and another for a different group.

- **Decide how many people you need to interview from each group.** This will depend on a number of factors. If the research project needs quantitative data, you need to be sure that the size of the sample will provide data which is valid and reliable. For qualitative projects, the sample will be much smaller. However, care needs to be taken to make sure that the make-up of the sample gathers information from all of the groups you need to contact.

- **Identify how you will contact the sample.** A sample is only useful if you can make contact with the people you want to be respondents. You need to plan precisely how to contact each group in the sample, to avoid problems later.

■ **Calculate how much it will cost to gather data from the sample.** Remember that there are many costs involved in gathering data. How much will you need to pay interviewers and/or moderators? If they need to travel to different places, how much do you need to cover expenses? How much will it cost to hire facilities for group discussions? If you intend to provide incentives for respondents, how much will they cost? Gathering data is likely to be one of the largest costs in your project, so you need to ensure you have enough money to put your sampling plan into action.

In this chapter, we looked at the key principles of sampling, and some of the major techniques used to identify an appropriate sample. It's important to remember that the accuracy and validity of the information gathered in a project depends on the researcher selecting a representative sample from the population of interest.

Selecting the best sample: case study

In Chapter 4, you thought about the best way to collect data to help the owners of T H Stores decide how best to extend their supermarket. The sample you choose for this project will depend on the research design and research methods you have already chosen.

The owners of the supermarket know that most of their customers live in the local area. However, some work nearby but live further away. On weekdays, there is a mixture of people who come in alone to buy small items such as sandwiches, schoolchildren who buy sweets, and mothers with small children who usually buy groceries. At weekends, more families come into the shop, and they tend to shop for a week's supply of food and household goods. The owners know they need to keep these customers, and attract new ones. They also know that the local council is concerned that small businesses in the area are being threatened by the growth of multinational stores, and that their suppliers are also keen to support local businesses.

Below are two research options which the owners have been considering. For each one, decide:

■ which different groups should be included in the sample;

■ which sampling method – or methods – should be used to select respondents from each group;

■ how you would contact the respondents in each group.

Option 1
A series of group discussions to gather views on how the store can best serve the local area.

Option 2
A questionnaire, administered by interviewers, to measure reactions to the owners' ideas of how to change the supermarket.

Compare your ideas with the suggestions on page 142.

Terminology test

The following research terms were introduced in this chapter. Can you explain what each one means?

- sample
- sampling plan
- quota
- reliability
- socio-economic group
- non-random sampling
- non-probability sampling
- interval sampling
- stratified random sampling
- disproportionate random sampling
- multi-stage sampling
- judgement sample
- snowball sample

- population of interest
- sample frame
- validity
- census
- random sampling
- probability sampling
- simple random sampling
- sampling interval
- proportionate stratified random sampling
- cluster sampling
- random route sample
- convenience sample

Summary

Effective research depends on the researcher choosing an appropriate sample. Don't forget that:

■ The sample should include respondents from the different groups in the population of interest. In some projects, the population of interest might include people who do not currently use or know about the client's products or services.

■ Quantitative data needs to be statistically valid and reliable. This means that the sample needs to be an accurate reflection of the population of interest, and larger than a sample for a qualitative project.

■ Sampling for qualitative projects also needs to reflect the population of interest. However, as qualitative research aims to uncover new ideas – rather than measure how widely held ideas are – researchers can use methods such as judgement, convenience and snowball sampling.

■ Sampling techniques fall into two main categories, probability (or random) sampling and non-probability sampling. The technique you choose will depend on the aim of the project, how much you know about the population – and how much money you have to spend.

■ It is very important to identify exactly how the sample will be contacted. Creating a sample with no plans about how to contact respondents can make the sample unusable.

Where can I find the data I need?

Using quantitative research methods

Introduction

In Chapter 3, you read about a range of different techniques for gathering data. Each technique can be used in a variety of ways, depending on the aim of the research project. In this chapter, we focus on the collection of quantitative data using these techniques – how and where it might be collected, and why it might be needed.

In this chapter, you will learn how to:

- describe the role and responsibilities of the market research interviewer in the data collection process;

- describe how data can be collected for different types of quantitative projects;

- identify the links between a chosen sampling method and a chosen data collection method;

- identify the practical constraints on the collection of data.

Quantitative data collection methods – a reminder

There are four main methods used to collect quantitative data:

■ face-to-face interviews;
■ telephone interviews;
■ self-completion questionnaires;
■ observation.

The first three methods involve questioning respondents directly, usually using a questionnaire. The last method – observation – involves watching people and commodities and analysing their movements. In this chapter, we look in more detail at how and why each might be used.

Interviewing in market research

What image springs to mind when you hear the phrase 'market research'? For many people, it is someone stopping people in the street and asking them to answer some questions. Market research interviewers are the very public face of market research, and their role is vital in ensuring that the data which is collected is accurate and valid.

Market research interviewers are the people who conduct quantitative interviews, either face-to-face or on the telephone. Their role is to make contact with people and persuade them to participate in a research project as a respondent. Once someone has agreed to participate, the interviewer has to administer the questionnaire and record the respondent's answers accurately, before returning the completed questionnaire to the research agency or department. At all points in the process, interviewers needs to ensure that they are conducting the interview and recording data ethically, and in line with data protection legislation. In the UK, MRS produces guidelines for interviewers to help them understand their ethical and professional obligations (www.mrs.org.uk/standards).

Being a market research interviewer

Who becomes an interviewer?
Interviewing tends to be part-time work, with companies having busy and less busy periods. Interviewers, therefore, are usually people who want to work part-time, to fit in with family life or other schedules.

What skills do I need to be an interviewer?
Interviewers need excellent interpersonal skills: the confidence to approach and engage potential respondents, and to administer the questionnaire in a way that makes the respondent feel

comfortable and happy to participate. At the same time, interviewers need to ensure that they don't influence the respondent's answers in any way, so it is very important to listen effectively. Organizational and administrative skills are also important, as well as an eye for detail when completing the questionnaire. Finally, interviewers need to be aware of the ethical and legal framework that governs their work. In particular, they need to ensure that they collect and record data in line with data protection legislation.

What qualifications do I need to be an interviewer?

There are no standard qualifications to become an interviewer. However, many research organizations offer a structured training programme for interviewers. In the UK, some organizations offer interviewers the opportunity to take the MRS Certificate in Interviewer Skills for Market & Social Research, a professional qualification specifically for experienced market research interviewers.

Where can I go to become an interviewer?

Some research organizations specialize in telephone interviews, while others organize a **field force** or large pool of face-to-face interviewers. You can find out about UK-based organizations which have telephone and field forces by visiting the Research Buyer's Guide website (www.rbg.org.uk).

In Chapter 4, we looked at the different ways a questionnaire could be used to collect data, including via interviews and via self-completion. We now look in more detail at how and why each approach might be used.

Collecting data using interviews

There are two main ways of conducting interviewer-administered interviews, either by telephone or face-to-face. Each has its own advantages for the research project.

Conducting telephone interviews

Telephone interviews are normally carried out from call centres, often using CATI equipment. If the interviewers are contacting respondents identified in a random sample, they will already have a list of the telephone numbers which they need to call. However, if a non-probability sampling approach is being used, a different way of selecting numbers is required. Often, telephone numbers are generated by a central computer, and interviewers call the number produced by the computer. The person who answers the call may match one of the profiles of respondents in the interviewer's quota. If so, he or she can be asked to participate in the survey, and the interviewer will lead him or her through the questionnaire. This process of generating a random telephone number in order to select respondents is called *random-digit dialling (RDD)*.

Organizing this collection of data by telephone from a central point (the call centre) has several benefits.

- **It can help interviewers reach wide geographical areas.** As a result, telephone interviewing is particularly popular for international research projects.

- **It can help keep costs down.** Face-to-face interviewers need to travel to meet respondents, and if they are working on a project with a random sample, they may have to return to a respondent's house more than once. They may also be interviewing at times or in places where not many people pass. As a result, they may not be able to make contact with many potential respondents. Telephone interviewers, on the other hand, can move quickly from one call to the next.

- **It makes it easier to monitor the quality of interviews.** Supervisors can listen in to interviews to make sure they are being carried out in line with interview guidelines, and that data is being recorded accurately.

- **It makes it easier and quicker to analyse data.** If data is recorded using CATI, it can be fed directly through *data processing* and analysis software. Although face-to-face interviews are increasingly conducted using computer equipment which can also allow this, a large proportion of surveys still use paper and pen interviewing (*PAPI*). Having to collect and process paper-based questionnaires adds more time to the project.

However, there are some limitations to using telephone interviews. For example, they are not suitable for projects where respondents need to look at materials or pictures, or try out products at the same time as completing the interview. It can also be difficult to conduct interviews on sensitive topics, such as health-related issues, by telephone. These types of interviews are therefore often carried out face-to-face.

Conducting face-to-face interviews

Face-to-face interviews can be carried out in a wide range of settings and for a wide variety of purposes. The list below shows some of the places you may encounter face-to-face interviews, and why they might be used.

- **In-home interviews.** Face-to-face interviews carried out in the respondents' own homes are very useful for longer sessions, where it is important for the respondent to feel relaxed. The interviewer also has the opportunity to demonstrate material or products and to get the respondents' immediate reactions. This type of interview is also particularly useful for projects where it is important to get the view of the whole family, and where companies wish to test new products for the home. For example, if a company is planning to launch a new clothes detergent to appeal to all the family, the interviewer might ask the respondent – and his or her family – to use the detergent for a week. One week later, the interviewer would return to the respondent's home to conduct a follow-up interview to collect their reactions to the product. This type of test – where the interviewer asks the respondent to try out the product – is known as a ***product test***. However, it is important to remember that, in some places, prospective respondents might be unwilling to admit an unknown interviewer to their home, and interviewers need to be very aware of personal safety when entering a stranger's house.

- **In-street interviews.** In the UK, it is not unusual to find teams of interviewers placed at intervals in town centres or other public areas. Projects using this approach to data collection usually use a quota sample, and depend on the interviewer to identify and approach people who appear to fit the quota. Like all other face-to-face techniques, in-street interviews allow interviewers to use support materials such as visual aids. As a result, they can be used to gather information on a very wide range of subjects. However, it is important that in-street interviews are kept short – respondents are unlikely to complete a long interview if they are standing outside in bad weather.

- **Hall tests.** In hall tests, respondents are invited to go to a specially designated area, such as a hall, a cordoned-off area of a supermarket or the reception room of a hotel, to participate in the interview. These interviews, known as ***hall tests*** (or central location tests), are particularly useful for testing products and administering longer questionnaires than can be used in in-street interviews. One popular use of hall tests is for ***taste tests,*** where respondents are asked to taste new food or drink products, and give their reactions.

- **Exit surveys.** Interviews are sometimes conducted outside stores or sports facilities, usually to determine what has been bought or done, or how the respondent felt about the store or about the facilities. These surveys are carried out when respondents leave the premises. ***Exit surveys*** are commonly used outside polling stations during elections to determine how people have voted.

Carrying out interviews: practice task

Look at the following examples of interviews being used to collect data. In each case, identify what type of interview is being used. Check your answers on page 142.

1. A mobile phone company wants to find out how well people understand phone companies' price plans. Teams of interviewers are placed outside railway stations and shopping centres to interview passers-by.

2. A national newspaper wants to find out how people in the country intend to vote in the forthcoming election. It has a team of people working in a call centre, calling potential respondents at home in the evening.

3. A soft drinks manufacturer wants to know if people prefer its new orange drink to its main competitors. Interviewers ask people shopping in the soft drinks aisle of a supermarket to go to an area just outside the supermarket to compare the taste of the two drinks.

4. A local council wants to know how residents in its area use the local health services. Interviewers visit residents in their houses to administer the questionnaire.

All interviews have important benefits for data collection. Skilled interviewers can make respondents feel that their views are highly valued, and can encourage them to respond to all questions, even if they have little time. As a result, they can obtain good response rates. Having enough members of the sample respond to the questionnaire is vital if the data is going to be valid and reliable.

However, telephone and face-to-face interviews can have some disadvantages. Face-to-face interviews, in particular, are expensive as the project costs need to include the interviewers' fees and travel expenses. Errors can also arise, even in the work of the most experienced interviewer. The most common types of error include:

◼ **Selecting respondents who don't fit the sample profile.** In quota sampling, in particular, interviewers need to screen potential respondents carefully. Failure to do so can have a major effect on the overall sample.

◼ **Omitting required information.** The MRS Code of Conduct stresses that respondents may opt out of an interview at any point. However, data from incomplete questionnaires may not be included in the final results, and interviewers who cannot persuade respondents to carry on until the end of the questionnaire put the results of the project at risk.

◼ **Failure to record data accurately.** Mistakes in the recording of information can have a major impact on the accuracy of the overall results.

Projects which have a limited budget may therefore opt to use self-completion questionnaires.

Collecting data using self-completion questionnaires

As we saw in Chapter 4, self-completion questionnaires can be delivered via a variety of media: e-mail, post or the internet. They can also be given directly to respondents, delivered as inserts in magazines and newspapers, or picked up by respondents in public places. This range of delivery mechanisms makes self-completion questionnaires popular for a very wide range of research projects. Here are just a few examples:

Customer satisfaction surveys

Self-completion questionnaires are widely used by companies to research their customers' opinions of the service they receive or the products the company produces. Hotels and restaurants often place short questionnaires in rooms and on tables as a way of continuously monitoring their customers' views.

Omnibus survey

Sometimes, companies may only need to commission a very limited amount of research – and they might not have a large research budget. For example, a new company producing specialty chocolate might want to find out which area of the country would provide the best market to test their product. Creating and sending out questionnaires to all areas of the country could prove very expensive. However, by adding their questions to an existing questionnaire, sent out by another company, the chocolate producers can get the information they need without commissioning a whole research project. This is the *omnibus* – a questionnaire which is made up of questions asked on behalf of a wide range of different companies.

Omnibus surveys are run by research agencies. The agency is responsible for the design of the questions and for collecting and analysing the data for each company that has bought space in the survey. The omnibus questionnaire may include questions asked on behalf of up to a dozen different companies. As a result, the questionnaires are usually very long and contain questions on a very wide range of subjects.

The most important advantages of using self-completion questionnaires to gather data relate to the cost of research. By delivering the questionnaire directly to the potential respondents, the researcher avoids interviewer costs, which can be very high. As a result, self-completion questionnaires are very popular for small projects which have very restricted budgets and where it is easy to contact a large pool of potential respondents. By contrast, they are also very popular for very large-scale projects, where extremely large numbers of respondents are required and where the costs and time involved in collecting the data using interviews would make the project unviable. An example of this is the national census in the UK, where a self-completion form is delivered by hand to each household in the country, and collected in person on a set date. By using personal delivery and collection, the researchers of the National Statistics Office can identify precisely any gaps in their information resulting from non-return of forms.

Although self-completion questionnaires appear to provide a very attractive, low-cost option for gathering data, there are some important limitations to their use:

■ **Who answered the questions?** Without an interviewer present, it is difficult to know precisely whose views have been given. For example, if a questionnaire is distributed in a magazine, it might not be the readers of the magazine who complete the survey. Instead, it could be other members of the family who do not fall into the target group. Being unable to screen out respondents who do not fit the sample require-ments limits the usefulness of self-completion questionnaires in projects which require very precise samples.

■ **Have all the questions been answered?** Interviewers must be skilled in encouraging respondents to answer all the questions in a questionnaire truthfully. With no interviewer present, respondents may simply omit questions which they think are unimportant or intrusive, or worse, give inaccurate answers. These are known as *respondent errors*. In order to minimize these, it is important that self-completion questionnaires are easy to follow, and that questions are devised in a way which encourages truthful answers.

■ **How will the data get back to the research organization?** As we saw in Chapter 4, relying on respondents to return questionnaires to the company can lead to low response rates. Although it might be possible to arrange for the collection of completed questionnaires, this is an expensive option. In order to get around these problems, many organizations offer incentives, such as prize draws, to encourage respondents to return questionnaires.

■ **How will the data be processed and analysed?** Like paper-based questionnaires completed by interviewers, completed self-completion questionnaires need to be reviewed carefully to check for errors before the answers are entered, by hand, into a computer program for analysis. This process of data processing can be time-consuming and expensive. It is important, therefore, that the researcher identifies exactly how the data will be processed when planning to use a self-completion questionnaire to collect data.

Many of the limitations of self-completion questionnaires have been overcome in recent years with the growth of data collection via the internet. Software packages allow questionnaires to be compiled and distributed, and data collected, quickly and easily.

Computer-assisted web-based interviewing (CAWI): interviewing or self-completion?

Online data collection has grown considerably in recent years. This is partly because new software packages enable companies to develop and distribute questionnaires, and analyse findings, quickly and easily. Although the packages can be expensive initially, once they are installed the company can use them for multiple projects, thereby reducing costs enormously. But how does CAWI work?

Potential respondents are usually invited by e-mail to complete a questionnaire by following a weblink. By using web technology, the research company can avoid some of the problems which can affect other types of self-completion questionnaires. For example:

■ In most online questionnaires, the programme ensures that respondents answer one question before moving to the next. This ensures that the respondents can't miss out questions.

■ Most online survey packages enable respondents to bypass questions that are not relevant to them. For example, if a respondent answers 'No' when asked if he or she has bought a particular product, the software will make sure he or she is not asked questions about when and where it was bought.

■ As the questionnaires are completed online, the data provided by the respondents can be fed immediately into analysis software. This means that projects can be completed much more quickly than with more traditional approaches.

Although respondents complete the questionnaire themselves, web-based questionnaires allow for a high level of interactivity, with the computer taking the place of the interviewer. This interactivity means that respondents can be guided more effectively through the questionnaire, just as they are in a face-to-face or telephone interview. As a result, although respondents complete the questionnaire themselves, this approach is known as *computer-assisted web interviewing (CAWI)*. It is important to remember, however, that this approach may exclude the people in the sample who have no access to the internet or who have limited IT skills.

Self-completion questionnaires: practice task

Before you complete this task, make a list of the different types of surveys that use self-completion questionnaires. These have been described in this chapter and in Chapter 4.

Now look at the following examples of research projects that have been designed to use self-completion questionnaires. In each case, identify the type of survey being carried out.

1. A local council wants to find out if its recent campaign to improve local services, such as street cleaning, rubbish collection and street lighting, has been successful. It has sent a questionnaire to all houses in the area, with a stamped, addressed envelope for respondents to return the completed questionnaire.

2. A hotel has placed short questionnaires in each bedroom, asking guests to give their opinions on the level of service provided. Guests leave their completed questionnaires in their rooms when they check out.

3. A government department is consulting small businesses on their opinions about a new scheme to promote learning in the workplace. A questionnaire is loaded onto its website, and an e-mail is sent to a sample of small businesses, inviting them to visit the site.

4. A large research organization has compiled a questionnaire with questions from 25 different retail companies. Copies of the questionnaire are included in the May edition of a woman's magazine. The questionnaire is designed to be folded by the respondent to show a return address and prepaid stamp, and to be posted back to the research organization.

Compare your answers with those on page 142.

Collecting data using observation

Collecting data about people by observing them rather than asking them questions can provide researchers with valuable information. Watching and recording the ways in which people behave and react can uncover patterns of behaviour of which the individuals concerned might not be conscious. As a result, observation can be a very useful tool for discovering exactly how people use goods and services, and can provide a useful complement to questionnaires and interviews. As we saw in Chapter 4, observation is useful for gathering either qualitative or quantitative data. In this section, we look at some common uses of observation in quantitative studies.

■ **Passenger surveys.** Many organizations, such as transport companies, need to know how many people use their services. For example, a bus company might need to know how many people get on and off its buses at particular stops. Passenger surveys, where the role of the researcher is to count the numbers of people getting on or off each train or bus, can help transport companies identify more precisely which areas of their services are most popular, and if additional buses or trains are required. This approach (of counting the people using a particular service) is widely used in other areas too. For example, a local council that runs sports facilities might count the numbers of people using those facilities at different times to find out if they are adequate to meet demand.

■ **Analysing CCTV footage.** As more retail stores and public areas are monitored by closed-circuit television, researchers have recognized the usefulness of the technology in finding out more about shoppers' habits. CCTV footage can reveal which areas of a shop are most popular, or how often a particular display encourages shoppers to stop and buy.

■ **Mystery shopping.** In Chapter 4, you were introduced to mystery shopping as a tool for researching customer service in retail organizations. This type of research, in which researchers pose as shoppers to record their experiences of customer service in shops or other service providers, is a popular approach to help measure the effectiveness of customer service training. For example, if a retailer has a set procedure that employees must follow when dealing with a customer's complaint, the mystery shopper might make a complaint then report on how well the employee followed the procedure.

Like all data collection methods, observation can have its limitations. Although it can be used to gather purely quantitative data (such as counting the people passing a particular place), it often involves some interpretation on the part of the researcher. For example, someone watching on a camera might see that a shopper has stopped at a particular point in a shop, but cannot be sure why without asking the person.

Collecting data by observation – what is ethical practice?

On pages 8–9, we discussed the guidelines interviewers need to follow to ensure they collect data ethically and legally. However, these guidelines don't apply only to interviews. Self-completion questionnaires must provide potential respondents with enough information to ensure that they understand the purpose of the research and what will be done with their data. In particular, they need to give their consent if the research organization wishes to use the data for anything other than the research project they are participating in. It is also important to understand the ethical constraints involved in observation. Just like respondents in interviews and those completing questionnaires, people being observed for research purposes need to know that research activity is taking place, and to have the right to opt out. For example, if an organization wants to use CCTV footage for research purposes, it should place a clearly visible sign in the area being recorded, telling passers-by how the footage will be used.

The MRS Code of Conduct provides very clear guidance on how data can be collected ethically and legally (www.mrs.org.uk/standards).

In this chapter, we have looked in more detail at the ways in which quantitative data can be collected, and at some of the strengths and limitations of each approach. We have also looked at some of the ethical constraints that govern the collection of data. When choosing a data collection method, it is important to consider all of these aspects to ensure that the method really is the most suitable for your project.

Collecting quantitative data: practice task

Look at the following examples of research projects which require quantitative data. Which data collection method would you suggest, and why? Remember, it is possible that different methods could be used to collect data from different groups within the sample.

1. Kitchen Gadgets is a company specializing in kitchenware, which it sells via a very popular website. It plans to introduce a new range of general homeware, called Living Gadgets. The company would like to know whether selling the new general homeware will take sales away from the kitchenware. It has the names, addresses, telephone numbers and e-mail addresses of its customers who have signed up in the stores to receive a catalogue.

2. A local health authority is concerned about the level of smoking-related illnesses that is being reported in hospitals in the area. The health authority has commissioned research in its local area to find out how aware smokers are of the risks involved in smoking, and whether a planned education campaign will encourage them to stop. The research will include showing the respondents pictures and samples of the education material, and asking them to rate their effectiveness.

Case study question

3. The owners of T H Stores know that their customers are attracted into their shop by the fresh fruit and vegetables near the door. However, they feel they could increase their sales if they understood more about how their customers move through the shop. In particular, they would like to know how to encourage customers to visit all areas of the shop.

Compare your answers with the suggestions on page 143. Remember that a number of different approaches might be suitable.

Terminology test

The following research terms were introduced in this chapter. Can you explain what each one means?

- field force
- product test
- taste test
- omnibus survey
- respondent error
- CAWI

- random-digit dialling (RDD)
- hall test
- response rate
- exit survey
- data processing
- PAPI

Summary

▨ Interviews, either face-to-face or on the telephone, can help encourage respondents to participate in research. A good interviewer can make respondents feel valued and can guide them effectively through the questionnaire.

▨ Self-completion questionnaires are usually cheaper to administer than those requiring an interviewer. However, care needs to be taken when designing the questionnaire to make sure that it is easy to complete and return.

▨ Online questionnaires provide a cost-effective option, as they provide the interactivity of interviewing with the ease of self-completion. However, it is important to check that the sample being contacted has easy access to the internet and is confident about responding online.

▨ Whichever approach to data collection you choose, you need to check how the data you need can be gathered ethically and legally. Remember to read the MRS Code of Conduct and to check the requirements of local data protection legislation.

How can I find out what people *feel* about issues?

Using qualitative research methods

Introduction

In Chapter 6, we looked at the different ways in which a researcher might gather quantitative data – that is, data that can provide statistics on how many people hold a particular opinion, or the strength of that opinion among the population. However, what happens when you do not know what types of opinions are held by the group you want to research? In this chapter, we look in more depth at how researchers can gather and analyse qualitative data in order to find out more about people's deeply held thoughts and opinions.

In this chapter, you will learn how to:

■ describe how qualitative data is used in market research;

■ describe the roles played and the skills required by the interviewer and moderator in gathering qualitative data;

■ describe some of the key tools and techniques used to collect qualitative data;

■ choose the best approach to gather qualitative data for a research project.

What is qualitative data, and why do we need it?

As we saw in Chapter 6, quantitative research allows organizations to gather information from large samples of a population of interest. By using structured questions with a range of predetermined answers to choose from, quantitative studies can count how many people hold the same opinions or beliefs. However, although people share the same opinion, they may have very different reasons for arriving at that opinion. Finding out why people make particular choices or think in particular ways is central to qualitative research.

Collecting qualitative data involves recording an individual's exact words and behaviour, then analysing what was said and done in great detail. By talking in depth with people, researchers can find out about their deeply held beliefs, and identify how new opinions might be taking shape. This qualitative data is important in market research because it helps organizations identify the roots of ideas and attitudes. The ideas may only have been expressed by a small number of people, but they can provide an important starting point for further, quantitative research.

How qualitative data can help solve business problems

Qualitative research plays different roles at different stages in the research process. At the beginning of a project, it can help keep research costs down by providing a focus for quantitative research. Talking in depth to a small number of respondents at the beginning of a project can:

- **Identify problems or ideas that need to be researched more fully.** For example, a college that wants to know why attendance on part-time courses for adults is falling might decide, in the first instance, to speak to a small number of current and former students. This can help identify potential roots of the problem.

- **Identify whether a market exists for a new product.** A publishing company might decide to launch a new magazine. Testing the idea at an early stage with a small group of readers first will help identify possible reactions and any major problems before the company moves on to wider development of the product.

- **Narrow down an organization's list of options.** A drinks manufacturer might want to launch a new range of fruit-flavoured drinks, and needs to know which flavours to offer. Qualitative research can help rule out any flavours that seem very unpopular.

- **Identify the range of opinions that exists about an issue so that the quantitative stage can measure how widespread they are.** An environmental charity might want to know about people's attitude to the environment. Qualitative research will identify the issues that need to be asked about in the quantitative stage.

- **Determine the important perceptions of a brand's image.** A car manufacturer might want to know how its brand is seen against other brands. First it needs to identify through qualitative research how its own and other brands are seen, so it can go on to measure the strength of the similarities and differences between them.

Qualitative research can also be carried out alongside, or following, quantitative research. Talking in depth to some respondents during or after a quantitative study can:

- **Help identify *why*** certain opinions appear to be strongly held. For example, a political party that discovers, through a survey, that many of its supporters intend to vote for a different party next time round might use qualitative research to find out more about why this is the case.

- **Help develop popular ideas more fully.** In Chapter 3, you read about publishers who were thinking of making changes to the format of their newspaper. One possible use for qualitative research which was discussed was the testing of a range of new ideas with groups of respondents, to find out how they would work in practice.

- **Provide more vibrant insight for a client.** Using word-for-word comments from respondents in a research project can help to illustrate findings for clients, and make the findings come to life.

Of course, many research projects involve only qualitative research. Where populations of interest are very small or hard to reach, it may not be feasible to carry out quantitative research. For example, research into the use of a new drug by medical specialists is likely to be qualitative since the drug company needs to fully understand the range of opinions and reactions among this specialized sample.

There are some problems with qualitative research, however, which can lead organizations to question its usefulness. The most common criticism is that the samples involved in qualitative research projects are usually quite small. As the interviewer needs to discuss issues in depth with the respondents, gathering data can take much longer than with quantitative projects. Furthermore, because the data is in the form of verbatim, or word-for-word, answers, the analysis stage can take much longer. As a result, it is not possible to interview as many people as can be interviewed using a structured questionnaire. This use of small samples of respondents, providing their own individual answers, means that qualitative data cannot provide the reliability that researchers aim to provide with quantitative research. We cannot be sure that, if we interview another group of people, they will provide the same answers to the questions asked. As a result, we cannot say that the data provided by qualitative research represents the views of the population as a whole.

However, qualitative research *does* provide extremely useful insight into thoughts and views which might otherwise remain hidden. In exploring the respondents' views in depth, the researcher can uncover highly valid information about some of the views held within the population of interest. As a result, although it will not show how many people hold a certain opinion, qualitative research can help identify a wider range of opinions than quantitative research. Unlike quantitative research, the questions asked are not fixed and a good researcher can identify unexpected themes of interest and explore them. This flexibility makes qualitative research ideal for exploratory research.

Qualitative data collection methods – a reminder

There are three main methods used to collect qualitative data:

■ depth interviews (also known as in-depth interviews);
■ discussion groups (also known as focus groups);
■ observation.

Whether data is gathered by talking with the respondents or watching and recording their behaviour, the aim of the qualitative researcher is always the same: to find out more about why people think or act in a certain way.

Moderating and conducting depth interviews

In Chapter 4, you read about the roles of the moderator and the depth interviewer in collecting qualitative data. In this section, we look in more detail at the skills that moderators and depth interviewers need in order to gather the information they need.

It is important to remember that the roles of depth interviewers and moderators are very different from those of interviewers in quantitative projects. Table 7.1 highlights some of the key differences.

Table 7.1 *Roles of quantitative and depth interviewers*

	Quantitative interviewers	Depth interviewers and moderators
Role in designing the project	None	The interviewer or moderator might also be the only researcher on the project. He or she might be responsible for designing the whole project.
Role in developing the questionnaire/ topic guide	Little or none. The questionnaire is designed by other departments and given to the interviewers.	High involvement, particularly in reviewing the topic guide to make sure it is meeting the research objectives
Role in interaction with the respondents	The interviewer reads the questionnaire to respondents as it is written and notes their answers. There is little or no room for the interviewer to ask unscripted questions.	The interviewer or moderator phrases his or her own questions, using the topic guide for guidance. The structure of the interview or discussion is under the control of the interviewer or moderator.
Role in recording information	The interviewer notes down responses on paper or on screen	The interviewer or moderator makes notes as the interview progresses, but also usually records the interview/discussion on audio or video tape.
Role in analysing data	None	The interviewer or moderator is usually closely involved in analysing the data, particularly if he or she is the only researcher on the project

As the table shows, those involved in moderating discussion groups or conducting depth interviews may also be responsible for other areas of the research project. Being closely involved at other stages in the project means that moderators or depth interviewers can develop a clear understanding of the research objectives, and can tailor their questions to meet the needs of those objectives.

Being an interviewer or a moderator in qualitative research

Who becomes an interviewer or a moderator?

Interviewers and moderators are usually skilled and experienced researchers. This is important because, unlike interviewers in quantitative projects, the role of the interviewers and moderators in qualitative research involves developing questions to make sure that the respondents provide data that is relevant to the research objectives. Like quantitative interviewers, however, the hours worked by interviewers and moderators can vary enormously, depending on their projects. As a result, they need to be prepared to work flexibly.

What skills do I need to be an interviewer or a moderator?

Interviewers and moderators need to have excellent interpersonal skills and must be expert in managing people and communication. This is particularly true when moderating discussion groups, when the moderator must ensure that the group dynamics are positive, that everyone in the group contributes, and that no one person dominates the discussion. Interviewers and moderators must be active listeners, identifying important points as they arise and steering the discussion to uncover the respondents' deeply held thoughts. To do this, they must also be able to establish a good rapport with respondents almost immediately, so that respondents feel comfortable talking about issues and feelings that might be sensitive or private. Like all researchers, they also need excellent organizational skills, and need to be fully aware of the ethical requirements that govern the conduct of depth interviews and discussion groups.

What qualifications do I need to be an interviewer or moderator?

There are no standard qualifications to become a moderator or interviewer. However, there are training programmes available. In the UK, the best-known courses are delivered by MRS (www.mrs.org.uk) and by the Association of Qualitative Researchers (AQR) (www.aqr.org.uk).

Where can I go to become an interviewer or moderator?

You can find out about UK-based organizations that specialize in qualitative research by visiting the Research Buyer's Guide website (www.rbg.org.uk). You can also visit the AQR website for further guidance.

Discussion group or depth interview – which is more useful?

In Chapter 4, we described the processes involved in conducting depth interviews and discussion groups. In this section, we look in more detail at why each is useful.

The benefits of discussion groups

Discussion groups can bring a number of benefits to a project. They can:

- **Provide a cost-effective way of gathering information.** Gathering respondents together in a group can help minimize the costs involved in collecting qualitative data. Groups normally consist of from 8 to 10 respondents, and may last one or two hours, so a great deal of information can be collected by the moderator.

- **Create a 'common language'.** When marketing a product, it is important for a company to understand how its customers talk about it. Discussion groups, with respondents talking together, allow the company to identify words and phrases used by potential customers when talking about the products – and to use these in marketing materials and in further research.

- **Generate a 'creative spark'.** By sharing ideas and thoughts, respondents may find they come up with brand new ideas. This makes discussion groups a good choice for projects such as naming new brands or developing new products.

- **Create a safe environment for discussion.** Groups may find that they share similar experiences or opinions, so may be more willing to talk about these together. For example, a project that is looking into the experiences of people who have HIV might find that discussion groups help sufferers share their thoughts more easily than one-to-one interviews.

- **Gather information from interaction.** As we saw in Chapter 4, observation is often used in qualitative research. Discussion groups not only provide the opportunity for people to talk about topics, but also allow the moderator the chance to watch how people interact with each other, and with any material that is provided. For example, the newspaper publisher discussed above might want to know what sections of the paper will be most popular. If the group is provided with sections of the new newspaper, the moderator can observe which ones draw most attention and how respondents react to the material.

- **Highlight sociological or cultural differences.** Companies need to know how different segments in society will react to their products or services. Discussion groups which bring together people from different segments – for example, teenagers and middle-aged adults, or people from different cultural backgrounds – can help spark discussion about how and why reactions might differ between groups.

There are some limitations to discussion groups, however. Not all respondents enjoy discussing issues with a group of strangers, particularly if the topic is sensitive or private. Not all groups 'gel' – put simply, some people may just not like each other. There is also always the chance that one person will try to dominate discussion or that others will be unwilling or unable to contribute. Although moderators are usually expert in creating a group rapport, these issues can make their work very difficult. As a result, depth interviews are particularly useful for some types of projects:

The benefits of depth interviews

Although they are usually more expensive to run than discussion groups, depth interviews have a number of advantages. They can be:

▪ **Easier to set up than discussion groups.** Discussion groups are held in special premises and participants need to be recruited (by the recruiter) in advance. Depth interviews can be easier to run because the interviewers can call at people's homes, or interview them at work. They might also conduct interviews by phone. As a result, depth interviews provide a more flexible approach to collecting qualitative data.

▪ **A safe environment for confidential or sensitive topics.** In a depth interview, respondents can be sure of complete confidentiality – there are no other group members who might repeat what was said in the interview. This is particularly important in projects where respondents might be worried that their views will not be kept private. For example, if a company is researching the possible impact that planned changes will have on its workforce, some employees may be reticent about letting their employer know their views. Depth interviews, with assurances of confidentiality, can help the researcher uncover how employees really feel.

▪ **An environment free from peer pressure.** We saw above that discussion groups are not ideal for all people. Some may not enjoy sharing their views in a group, particularly if they don't agree with the majority opinion. A clear example of this might be research into children's tastes in television programmes. If the majority of children dislike a certain programme, it's unlikely that an individual child will disagree with them. Speaking to the children outside their peer group can help give them the confidence to express their own, individual opinion.

▪ **Useful when interviewing hard-to-reach individuals.** Some people are notoriously hard to contact. This is particularly true of senior managers in businesses, where appointments might be booked months in advance. Using depth interviews in this type of situation means that the interview can be scheduled to fit in with the manager's diary.

▪ **Useful for gathering individual or specialist insight.** In some projects, it is important to know the views of specialists or individuals. For example, a manufacturer of specialized medical equipment might need to know the range of views of the specialists who use the equipment. Depth interviews will allow each specialist to give detailed information about how he or she uses – or might use – the equipment.

■ **Useful for gathering ideas from families, friends or co-workers.** In Chapter 4, we looked at some variations on depth interviews, such as duos and trios. By interviewing people together, such as family members or friends, it is possible for the interviewer to observe how the respondents normally interact around a product. For example, a confectionery company that is considering changing the range of chocolates in a box might need information on how people share its current boxes of chocolates. By talking with people who normally share chocolates – such as family groups – they can find out how to balance the selection in the new boxes.

Depth interviews do have some disadvantages. It is expensive and time-consuming both to run the interviews and to analyse the resulting data. A one-hour group discussion might provide information from between 8 and 10 respondents, while a one-hour depth interview might provide information from only one. However, the recording – and the transcript – for each will be of equal length. When planning a project using depth interviews, it is vital to allow enough time – and money – for the data to be analysed in depth.

Depth interview or discussion group? Practice task

Each of the projects described below needs qualitative data. In each example, decide which approach is best, depth interviews or discussion groups. Make notes about the reasons for your choice.

1. A cosmetics company is about to launch a new aftershave. It needs to find a name and marketing ideas that will appeal to its target market: men aged 18 to 30.

2. A health authority is investigating how best to help teenagers with mental illness. It wants to find out the views of young adults who have now recovered from a range of mental problems. It has a list of all of its former patients.

3. A large company is about to buy some new IT equipment, including printers and photocopiers, for its offices across the country. First, however, it needs to understand more about the ways in which its employees share their current resources and any ideas they have for making best use of the new equipment.

Compare your answers with the suggestions on page 143. Remember that a number of different approaches might be suitable.

Tools and techniques for depth interviewers and moderators

In Chapter 4, you read about the topic guide, the key tool used in discussion groups and depth interviews to guide respondents' discussions. Unlike a questionnaire, the topic guide does not provide a script which the interviewer or moderator must follow word-for-word. Instead, it provides a structure and prompts to help elicit the type of information which is needed.

Creating an effective topic guide

Before starting the process of data collection, interviewers and moderators need to develop the topic guide. During the first interviews or discussion groups, the interviewer or moderator will make notes about the usefulness of the topic guide, and may revise it for later interviews or groups. But what are the features of a good topic guide?

■ **Does the first stage provide reassurance for respondents?** All interviews or discussion groups should begin with a phase designed to put the respondents at ease. The topic guide may contain prompts to remind the interviewer or moderator to explain the purpose of the research, ensure that all the respondents understand how the information will be recorded and used, and ask some general questions about the respondents.

■ **Do the following stages cover all the research objectives?** The aim of the interview or discussion is to gather relevant information for the research project. The topic guide may contain clear groups of questions or prompts, each related to a specific research objective.

■ **Are sensitive or specific questions worded clearly?** Although the topic guide may include only prompts for most of the areas to be discussed, it might be necessary to include some scripted questions, particularly if there are very specific points which must be discussed.

■ **Does the topic guide bring the discussion to a close?** As well as providing support for the opening of discussion, the topic guide should help the interviewer or moderator bring it to a close. This includes making sure that the respondents have an opportunity to add any additional information, and that they are reminded of their rights as respondents.

When teams of moderators or interviewers are working on the same project, it is important that there are opportunities for them to compare how they are using the topic guide and to discuss any difficulties which have arisen. This helps to ensure an appropriate level of consistency across the discussion groups or interviews.

The topic guide provides a reminder for the interviewers and moderators of the issues that need to be discussed. However, respondents may be asked to talk about topics that they have never discussed before, such as how they feel about a particular product. To help respondents develop and talk about their ideas, interviewers and moderators can use a variety of techniques and materials.

Using projective techniques

Projective techniques is the name given to a collection of techniques that help the respondent to imagine a situation. For example, in the exercise above, you read about a company which is about to launch a new aftershave. It needs to gather the thoughts of consumers about this new product – but, as the product is so new, the respondents cannot say from experience how they feel about it. However, projective techniques allow the respondents to project themselves into a new situation, and to give an opinion about how people might feel. Projective techniques include:

- **Sentence completion.** Respondents should complete sentences in their own words, for example, 'Men who wear this aftershave are ...'

- **Brand personalities.** Respondents are asked to say or write down who a brand would be if it came to life, and then explain their choice: for instance, if this brand were a footballer (or a football team), who would it be?

- **Collages.** Respondents put together collages representing different brands from pictures supplied by the moderator.

Using stimulus material

Like projective techniques, stimulus material helps respondents formulate ideas and give opinions on new topics which they may not have considered before. Stimulus material is the name given to the wide range of materials which interviewers and moderators can use to stimulate ideas and discussion. Much of this material is visual – such as pictures and diagrams – but it also includes objects, such as test packaging, as well as sounds and smells. They might even ask the respondents to draw their thoughts. So, in our example of the new aftershave, the moderator or interviewer might use photos of different times of day or different places to see which ones respondents associate most closely with the fragrance, or they might use samples of the fragrance itself and ask respondents to draw whatever they think of when they smell the aftershave.

When projective techniques and stimulus material are included in depth interviews and discussion groups, the topic guide should indicate clearly when and why they are being used.

Encouraging respondents to talk: practice task

A major car manufacturer is about to launch a brand new model of small car. These examples are taken from discussion groups designed to find out what drivers think of the new car. Look at these examples of projective techniques and stimulus materials in action. In each example, try to identify the technique that is being used.

1. The moderator asks respondents to answer the question, 'If this car were an animal, what animal would it be?'

2. The moderator gives the respondents a selection of different fabrics. They must choose the one that most reminds them of the car, and say why.

3. The moderator plays an audio recording of the car being driven along a country road. Respondents have to say the first words they think of when they hear the sound of the car.

4. The moderator gives the respondents a series of images cut from a range of magazines, and asks them to create a picture that best represents their feelings about the car.

Compare your answers with those on page 143.

Collecting qualitative data using observation

In Chapter 6, we looked in detail at how observation could be used to collect quantitative data. However, observing how people behave can provide a great deal of qualitative data too. Observation is an important tool for qualitative researchers because, in many cases, what people do and what they say they do may be very different. For example, in a project focusing on the spending habits of young women, a respondent might say she goes shopping for clothes once every two to three months. However, if a researcher observed the respondent, he or she might find that she goes once every two to three weeks. Respondents may have a wide range of reasons for not giving accurate information. For example they might want to give the researcher a good impression of themselves, or they might not even be aware of their behaviour.

Observation is a key tool in helping uncover and describe respondents' true behaviour. Here are a few of the common ways of using observation techniques to collect qualitative data:

■ **Accompanied shopping.** This type of data collection is useful for retailers who want to find out what attracts respondents in their shop. A researcher accompanies the respondent as he or she shops, asking questions along the way. For example, the researcher might ask respondents to explain why they have stopped at a particular display, or why they have picked up a particular item.

■ **Ethnographic studies.** In these studies, the researcher might live or work with the respondent or respondents for a period of time – perhaps a few weeks or months.

Such studies provide an intensive period of observation, and are very useful for social research into the lives of different groups within society.

▦ **Respondent diaries.** Observation can be carried out by the respondent as well as the researcher. By asking respondents to record their thoughts and behaviour in a diary, the researcher can find out not only what respondents did, but how they felt about it. Projects that look at how to change behaviour – such as the local council's efforts to introduce a recycling scheme, which you read about in Chapter 5 – can learn a lot from respondents noting their own change in behaviour, and how they feel about it.

In this chapter, we have looked in more depth at the work of depth interviewers and moderators, and the tools and techniques that researchers use to gather qualitative data. Don't forget that the choice of method will depend to a great extent on the topic being researched. Qualitative research often focuses on sensitive issues or deeply held beliefs, and respondents need to feel secure before sharing their views with an interviewer or moderator.

Developing a topic guide: case study

In Chapter 5, you were asked to identify a sample for discussion groups focusing on the development of T H Stores. The owners have now decided they would like to conduct three discussion groups, two with customers and one with non-customers, to find out what they might like to see in the new store.

What topics do you think should be covered in the discussion? Try to plan a topic guide for the discussions with customers.

Compare your answer with the suggestion on pages 143–44. Remember that a number of different approaches might be suitable – each has its own strengths and limitations.

Terminology test

The following research terms were introduced in this chapter. Can you explain what each one means?

▦ projective techniques   ▦ stimulus materials

▦ ethnographic study   ▦ accompanied shopping

Summary

Qualitative information has a very important role to play in helping researchers explore the behaviour and motivations of respondents. However, great care needs to be taken to ensure that the information is valid:

- The role of the interviewer or moderator is very different from that of the interviewer in quantitative studies. Depth interviewers and moderators need to be skilled researchers who can both elicit and analyse data.

- Respondents will often be asked to reveal thoughts or ideas that they might not be conscious of. The skilled interviewer/moderator needs to make them feel comfortable enough to express these thoughts.

- A well-structured topic guide is essential to ensure that the discussion relates to the research objectives. When teams of interviewers or moderators are working together, they need to ensure they are all covering the same issues in similar ways.

- Projective techniques and stimulus materials can help respondents be creative and explore their own thoughts more deeply.

- Observation also has a key role to play in qualitative research. It can help identify differences between the respondents' words and behaviour.

What questions should I ask?

Designing the questionnaire

Introduction

In a quantitative study, once you know how you are going to collect the information, who you are going to interview, and have clearly defined your objectives, you can begin to design the questionnaire. Your aim is to design questions that provide you with the unbiased and accurate information you need, in a way which is appropriate for your chosen data collection method.

In this chapter, you will learn how to:

- decide what questions you need to ask;
- write questions to give you the most accurate and unbiased answers;
- order the questions to produce accurate and unbiased information;
- lay out the questionnaire to make it simple for everyone to use;
- pilot the questionnaire to ensure that it works;
- avoid common problems when creating questionnaires.

Getting the best information

The objective in writing the questionnaire is to get the best information that you can from your respondents. You must recognize that it will rarely be completely accurate. When asked how they behave, what they do and what they buy, respondents will often have to rely on memory, which may not be accurate. For example, when asked what they think of something, they may not already have a clear view and will tell you what they think at that moment. This may not be the same as they think at another time. When asked to predict if they will buy a new product, they can only give a best guess as to whether or not they will. Their future actions are likely to depend on other circumstances that they cannot take into account in the interview. One of the questionnaire writer's key jobs is to help respondents answer as accurately and as honestly as possible by asking questions that they can answer.

Stages of questionnaire design

The process of questionnaire design involves five clear stages:

1. Decide what you need to ask.
2. Create appropriate questions to cover all the areas you need to investigate.
3. Ensure the questionnaire flows well.
4. Lay out the questionnaire to assist completion.
5. Pilot the questionnaire to make sure it works.

In the following section, we look at each stage in turn.

Stage 1: Deciding what you need to ask

The first stage should always be to revisit the research objectives and determine what information you need to collect in order to be able to address them. These areas of information form the *information objectives*. A survey using a structured questionnaire can only collect information on points that have been identified at questionnaire design stage. If an important point is missed at this stage, the questionnaire will not collect data that relates to it. Determining exactly what information you need before you write the questionnaire is crucial.

For example, if the research objective for a sports clothing company is to determine the position of its brand in the market, its information objectives might be to find out:

◼ How well known is the brand?

◼ How often do people buy this brand, and where from?

- How is the clothing seen (for instance, as sports clothes or fashion clothes)?
- How is the brand name viewed by respondents?
- How does it compare with other brands?
- What is the image of this brand compared with other brands?

Stage 2: Creating appropriate questions

Questions need to be designed to address the information objectives. However, they also need to take into account a range of ethical requirements, primarily related to the rights of respondents to have their views accurately represented. When designing questions, therefore, there are a number of areas to consider.

Question content

Each question in the questionnaire serves a very specific purpose, gathering information that is directly relevant to the information objectives. All questions should also be easy for interviewers to ask and respondents to answer. Therefore, questions need to be clear and concise, with each focusing on a specific and separate issue. Asking about two issues in one question will result in faulty data. For example, if the sports clothing questionnaire asks, 'Do you think the clothes are comfortable and well-made?', it will not be clear whether a 'Yes' answer means 'Yes, comfortable' or 'Yes, well-made'. Make sure that each question addresses one area only.

Question wording

Wording questions appropriately is a skill which it takes time to develop. Badly worded questions can confuse respondents and may bias their responses. Always ensure that the vocabulary chosen for the questions matches the required audience. For example, a car manufacturer may use more technical terms when researching the views of mechanics than when researching the customers. It's also vital to avoid any ambiguous terms or responses. Take time to check that the question and the possible responses can only be interpreted in one way. Finally, make sure that the question does not lead the respondent to an expected answer. Questions should always be balanced so as not to suggest that there is a right or wrong answer. For example, if you want to know whether someone agrees with something, you should ask, 'Do you agree or disagree that …?' Asking only, 'Do you agree …?' might lead the respondent simply to say 'Yes', without considering other options. You could add, 'Or do you have no opinion about this?' so as not to force an opinion where none is held.

Question type

When you don't know how respondents are likely to answer or you want to record their answers in their own words, you should use an open-ended question. This is often used for questions that ask why or how, where you want to find out exactly what people say. When large numbers of people are interviewed, however, these answers need to be condensed and summarized for the analyst to make sense of them. This is a time-consuming and often costly process, so open-ended questions are usually kept to a minimum.

Most questions in a questionnaire are pre-coded. This means that there is a list of possible answers which the questionnaire writer has already compiled, and the respondent must choose one of these. Often a pre-coded question will only have two possible answers, usually Yes or No. This is known as a *dichotomous question*. However, some questions may have a longer list of possible answers. This list may be shown to the respondent to select an answer from, in which case it is a *prompted question*, or it may not be shown and used only for the interviewer to record the answer, making it an *unprompted question*. Where the questionnaire is self-completion, either paper or internet based, then all pre-coded questions are also prompted questions, as the respondent can see the range of answers. Keeping the prompt list exactly the same between questions wherever possible avoids confusing both the respondent and the interviewer and leads to fewer errors. Finally, don't forget that respondents might be unable to answer a question. Providing a 'don't know' option is vital if the questionnaire is to provide accurate data.

Measuring the response

Scales are a useful way of recording responses. The most commonly used types of scale include:

■ Numeric scales, where the respondent is asked to give a number, often out of 10, in order to rate how he or she feels about something.
■ Itemized rating scale, where the respondent has to choose one of a series of statements that are graded, perhaps from 'I would be very likely to buy it' to 'I would be very unlikely to buy it.'
■ Attitudinal rating scales, where respondents are asked to say how much they agree or disagree with a statement that expresses a particular attitude.

When using a semantic scale (that is, a scale that uses words rather than numbers), it is important to have as many items expressing a negative point of view as expressing a positive one. Having an imbalance in the scale can bias the results towards the view with the larger number of statements.

Scales are vital for quantitative research because they allow respondents to express the degree to which they hold a view, as well as providing a high level of consistency across questions. Consistency in the way in which answers are recorded across different questions can be helpful in the analysis process.

Getting the questions right: practice task

Look at the following questions taken from different questionnaires. Each has at least one major fault. Can you identify the problem with each question?

1. Are you happy with the range and usefulness of our products? (Yes/No)

2. Is it your intention to undertake any major renovations to your place of residence in the near future? (Yes/No)

3. Do you agree that it is not a good idea for smoking to be banned in public places? (Yes/No)

Compare your answers with those on page 144.

Stage 3: Ensuring the questionnaire flows well

There are several points to bear in mind when putting the completed questions in order to form the questionnaire.

■ **Make sure that the flow is logical.** It is important that the questionnaire is planned so that it has a flow. To help respondents to understand the questions and to give their best answers, the questions should not jump around between different topics, but follow a clear path. The aim should be to have a conversation with respondents that they can follow.

■ **Beware of prompting the respondent's thoughts.** It's also vital that questions are ordered so that they don't prompt respondents with the answers to questions that are going to come later. So, for example, if you want to find out which brand someone associates with a particular advertising slogan, you must make sure that you don't ask any earlier questions that give this answer away.

■ **Go from general to specific.** A questionnaire will normally go from general questions about the topic to more detailed questions about a specific area, brand or product. Detailed questions about the area being researched normally come towards the end of the questionnaire. For example, if you are researching respondents' reactions to a particular brand of soft drink, placing questions about the specific brand early in the questionnaire will bring it to the forefront of the respondent's mind. This will, in turn, give the brand an advantage in any later questions where brands are compared, or in questions about which brands the person buys. Many surveys seek to establish what products or brands people can think of, before asking about specific brands. To do this, we can use *spontaneous questions*. Such questions include:
  – What brands of coffee can you think of?
  – For which opticians have you seen any advertising on television recently?
  – Please give me as many makes of Japanese cars as you can think of.

These questions give respondents a chance to search their memories, and can help show how effective advertising has been. However, it should be noted that some respondents may guess who the research is being carried out for, and this could affect the answers they give. The responses to these later questions will be subject to *bias*, as the questionnaire has dictated how the respondent is going to think.

You need to plan the questionnaire so that spontaneous questions always come before any prompted questions that help respondents with their answers.

■ **Think carefully about what classification questions you need to ask.** *Classification questions* are questions that are not directly about the subject of the survey, but seek personal details of the respondent or their household that you need for analysis purposes. For consumer surveys they commonly include:
- age of respondent;
- gender of respondent;
- social grade;
- household composition, including number and ages of children;
- working status;
- amount of television watched;
- newspapers read.

For business-to-business surveys they might include:
- nature of business, or standard industrial classification (SIC) code;
- turnover of company;
- number of employees;
- job title of respondent;
- age of respondent;
- trade journals read.

Because classification questions do not relate directly to the subject of the interview, they can be seen as intrusive and unnecessary. As a result, they usually appear at the end of the questionnaire. Sometimes, however, they form part of the recruitment process, for example if the researcher is only looking for people within certain age groups. In this case, the relevant questions must be asked at the beginning of the interview. Wherever they are included, it's important to include only questions that are vital to the information objectives. For example, in a business-to-business survey, ask yourself whether personal details of the respondent's age are going to increase your understanding of the findings before including them.

Creating a logical questionnaire: top tip

Producing a flow chart of the questions can be a good aid to planning, particularly where the questionnaire is computer-based.

Stage 4: Laying out the questionnaire to make it user-friendly

Laying out the questionnaire is extremely important whatever type of data collection method is used.

- **Provide clear routing through the questionnaire.** In all but the most straightforward questionnaires, you are likely to encounter *question routing*. Routing dictates which questions respondents should answer next, where this depends on their answer to the previous question. Clear routing should help respondents avoid questions that are not relevant to them. With paper-based questionnaires, question routing should be kept as simple as possible to prevent the interviewer or the respondent (if self-completion) from making mistakes and answering the wrong questions. With computer-based techniques, the routing is automatic and hidden from the interviewer and the respondent. It can therefore be more complex, with responses to several questions being taken into account. However, computer-based questionnaires need careful and extensive checking to ensure that all possible routes through the questionnaire work properly.

- **Help the interviewer to do his or her job well.** Interviewer-administered questionnaires need to contain all the instructions that the interviewer requires to successfully complete the interview. This means that any instructions about routing need to be clear and easy to follow.

- **Think about what the questionnaire looks like.** Self-completion questionnaires need to be attractive, to encourage the respondent to complete them, and easy to follow, so that few mistakes are made. Remember that, if the questions and the routing are difficult to follow, or if the questionnaire looks boring, the respondents are less likely to spend their time completing it.

- **Think about where the codes go.** As we mentioned above, many questions in a questionnaire are pre-coded. This means that each question and each possible answer is represented by a unique number, or code. The codes are used to aid the processing of the data during the analysis stage, and we look at this in more detail in Chapter 9. In online questionnaires, this coding is hidden from the respondent. However, in paper-based questionnaires, the codes are usually included on the questionnaire itself. It is important to think about how these are shown. If they are too prominent on a self-completion questionnaire, they may distract or confuse the respondent. If they are too small on an interviewer-administered questionnaire, the interviewer might not be able to see them easily to aid coding. Think carefully about who will complete the questionnaire when laying out the coding.

Labelling the questionnaire: practice task

Look at this extract taken from an interviewer-administered questionnaire as part of a survey into people's reading habits, then answer the questions below.

Question 6: Which daily newspapers can you think of? [Do not read list to the respondent. Indicate all which respondent mentions.]

The Sun	[1]
The Times	[2]
The Daily Express	[3]
The Guardian	[4]
The Telegraph	[5]
Other (please specify).................................	

Question 7: Do you read a newspaper on a daily basis?

Yes	[1]
No	[2]

If 'Yes', go to Question 8. If 'No', go to Question 9.

Question 8: Which newspaper or newspapers do you buy on a daily basis? [Do not read list to the respondent. Indicate all which respondent mentions.]

The Sun	[1]
The Times	[2]
The Daily Express	[3]
The Guardian	[4]
The Telegraph	[5]
Other (please specify).................................	

Figure 8.1 *Questionnaire extract*

In the extract, find examples of:

1 a dichotomous question;

2 an unprompted question;

3 routing instructions;

4 response codes.

Compare your answers with those on page 145.

Stage 5: Piloting the questionnaire to make sure it works

A pilot survey is carried out to test the questionnaire with a small group of people and revise it wherever necessary so that the final questionnaire works better. The pilot survey can help answer a number of questions about the questionnaire. These include:

▪ Do respondents understand the questions as you meant them to be understood?

▪ Are the answer codes provided adequate to record the responses accurately?

▪ Does the interview or questionnaire hold the interest of the respondents or do they get bored?

▪ If the questionnaire is interviewer-administered, does the interviewer understand the questions and read them out as you intended?

■ If it is interviewer-administered on paper, can the interviewer follow the routing instructions?

■ If it is administered on computer, does the routing work as you intended?

■ How long does it take to complete?

It is possible to pilot the questionnaire in a number of ways:

■ **A mock interview with a colleague or friend pretending to be a respondent** can be sufficient to identify problems in the questions and the routing instructions.

■ **A small number of interviews with eligible respondents**, during which you observe their reaction, followed by a discussion of the questionnaire with them. You may ask what they understood by certain questions, particularly those where you saw that they had difficulty, and what they intended their answers to mean. This can ensure that you have adequately captured the respondents' answers, particularly where you have provided pre-codes.

■ **A larger scale pilot where you interview possibly 50 or more people** and tabulate the answers to find out whether you have questions with high levels of 'don't know' response. This can indicate a problem with the question. You can also find out if there are pre-coded questions with a high proportion of answers written in because the list of items you have provided is incomplete or insufficient.

Piloting is a vital stage, ensuring that the questionnaire will produce the accurate and unbiased information you need.

Some common problems with questionnaires, and how to avoid them

As you have seen, questionnaire design can be quite a complex task. However, when done properly, it can provide you with an extremely useful tool for measuring respondents' views. Taking time to design the questionnaire appropriately can save time and money in the long run, as you are sure that the information you have is both accurate and unbiased.

In addition to following the stages above, however, there are some important dos and don'ts to bear in mind when designing a questionnaire:

Do

■ **Think about what the respondent needs to know.** When people are approached to take part in the survey, the introduction that is usually written on the questionnaire is crucial both to gaining their cooperation and in how they feel about having taken part in the survey. They should be told:

– the name of the interviewer;
– a broad indication of the subject matter of the survey;
– the length of time that the interview is likely to take.

▦ **Ask respondents about what they know.** Ensure that the person you are interviewing is the right person to answer the question. For example, if you ask a mother how many hours a week her teenage son spends playing video games, you are unlikely to get an accurate answer. Make sure that the question suits the respondent it was designed for.

▦ **Be aware of *social desirability bias*.** This occurs when respondents say they do something or think something which they don't actually do or think because:

– they want to impress the interviewer;
– they feel that what they really do or really say is not socially acceptable;
– they fool themselves into thinking that this is what they really do.

Thus, for example, they might tell you that they:

– have a more expensive car or watch than they really do;
– always give the money back in a shop if someone gives them too much change;
– take exercise more often than is actually the case.

Identify questions that may be subject to social desirability bias and ask them sensitively or in several different ways.

▦ **Respect the respondent's rights.** The information collected can only be used for the purposes to which the respondent has agreed, and you cannot identify respondents to anyone without their agreement, except for purposes of survey administration. If interviews are to be recorded, either voice or video, respondents must be told this beforehand. The recording cannot be used for any purpose other than that for which permission is gained. Asking for permission should therefore be included in the questionnaire.

Don't

▦ **Expect respondents to have perfect recall.** Don't expect people always to accurately remember what they did or when they bought something. Respondents are likely to remember large purchases, such as a car, but not smaller ones, such as everyday food items. Therefore, tailor your questions to how likely respondents are to remember the details. For more accurate purchasing information of household items, panels of people are used who record daily what they buy.

▦ **Mislead respondents about how long it will take to complete the interview or questionnaire.** It is important to be honest about the likely length of the interview. It is not always possible to be precise because the number of questions asked may depend on the answers given. However, it can be tempting to suggest that the interview or questionnaire will be shorter than it is in order to get the cooperation of the respondent. This, though, is unwise. The respondent might withdraw midway through the interview when it becomes obvious that it will be longer than he or she expected. The interviewer has then wasted not only the respondent's time, but his or her own time as well. And, as a result, the respondent is less likely to agree to take part in future surveys.

▧ **Give too much information about the aims of the survey.** The respondent should be told the broad nature of the subject matter of the survey. However, too detailed a description may bias responses or give a bias to the type of people who agree to be interviewed. For example, if you say that a survey is about store loyalty schemes, then people who are not interested in store loyalty schemes are more likely to refuse to be interviewed than people who have store loyalty cards. This is not a problem if you are only looking for loyalty card users, but if you want to interview non-users as well, they could be under-represented in the sample.

Is your questionnaire ethical?

The MRS Code of Conduct provides very clear guidance on the rights of respondents and how questionnaires should be designed and delivered to respect these rights. MRS has also produced guidelines on good practice when designing questionnaires. The Code of Conduct and the questionnaire design guidelines can be found on the MRS website (www.mrs.org.uk).

Designing a questionnaire: case study

Following the discussion groups with customers, the owners of T H Stores would like to find out how popular some of the ideas which were suggested in the discussions might be. They have asked the researcher to develop a questionnaire to gather quantitative data. They intend the questionnaire to be administered by a small team of interviewers in the shop and in the surrounding area.

One of the owners of T H Stores has become very interested in research and has tried to develop some questions for the questionnaire (see below). However, there are some problems with the questions he has devised. Look at the extract below and make notes about the problems.

Question 9: How often do you shop at T H Stores?
1. Once a day
2. Once a week
3. Once a month
4. Never

Question 10: Which aspects of shopping at T H Stores do you like best?
1. The friendly staff
2. The wide range of fresh food
3. The convenience of having a shop close to home

Question 11: Which shops do you shop at regularly?
1. T H Stores
2. Tesco
3. Sainsbury
4. Waitrose

Question 12: Do you agree that it's a good idea to expand T H Stores?
Yes / No

Figure 8.2   *Questionnaire extract*

Compare your answers with the suggestions on page 145.

Terminology test

The following research terms were introduced in this chapter. Can you explain what each one means?

- information objectives
- dichotomous question
- unprompted question
- spontaneous question
- question routing
- social desirability bias
- pre-coded question
- prompted question
- bias
- classification question
- pilot survey

Summary

The questionnaire is crucial in quantitative research. The wrong questions or badly written questions can give you incomplete or misleading results. To avoid this:

- determine what information you need to collect in order to answer the research objectives;

- write clear, unbiased questions that are easy to be asked and to be understood;

- ask about one thing only in a question;

- ask questions that the respondents can answer;

- plan the questionnaire to make it logical and easy to follow;

- make sure that any routing works;

- pilot the questionnaire before you use it in the main survey.

Completing a market research project

9

How do I know what it all means?

Analysing research data

Introduction

With the interviews completed, you need to bring the data together and analyse it. This involves organizing the data into an appropriate format for your method of analysis, and then trying to work out what it means.

In this chapter, you will learn how to:

- organize quantitative data for analysis;
- specify quantitative data analysis;
- interpret quantitative data;
- analyse qualitative data.

Organizing quantitative data

Before analysis can begin, it's important to organize the data into a format that can be manipulated easily. The first stage in this organization process is to identify how the respondents answered the questions.

Pre-coded questions: a reminder

As we saw in Chapter 8, questions included in structured questionnaires normally have a set of pre-coded responses for respondents to choose from. When a survey is carried out with a large number of respondents, these pre-coded responses provide an important aid to analysis. They make it possible to use computer analysis programs to analyse responses and to produce tables of data from those responses.

In order to analyse the responses, each pre-coded answer is given a unique code by which it can be identified. The format of these codes depends on the analysis program that is to be used, and the codes need to be included on the questionnaire. If the codes for all the responses chosen by each respondent are entered into the program, it is possible to produce tables showing how the sample of respondents answered each question.

One advantage of computer-based questionnaires is that the coding is embedded within the program. This means that each answer can be identified automatically, and tables of data can be available almost immediately.

It is important to remember, however, that questionnaires may also include open-ended questions. The responses to these questions present some challenges to the researcher.

Coding open-ended questions

With an open-ended question, where the answers have been written or typed in verbatim, there are no predetermined codes. In order to analyse these answers, a *code frame* needs to be produced. To do this, a sample of up to 100 verbatim responses to the question are extracted and similar answers are grouped. Where a number of respondents give essentially the same answer to a question, a code is created for that answer. A list of codes for all the commonly occurring answers is then created. This is the code frame. All the questionnaires are then read again and codes from this code frame are allocated against the answers given.

Once the coding is complete, the data needs to be processed.

Processing the data

There are several stages involved in *processing data* that has been recorded on paper-based questionnaires. First, the data needs to be entered on to a computer for analysis. This *data entry* may be done manually, using a keyboard, or by optical scanning.

Once it is entered into the computer program, the data needs to be edited to ensure that the respondent has answered the right questions, and to check for inconsistencies in individual respondent's answers. Paper questionnaires can be edited before the data is entered. However, *data editing* often takes place after the data has been entered into the program. Common edits include:

- rectifying out-of-range data values, such as a code of 7 when only codes 1 to 5 have been used;

- identifying an answer to a question that should not have been answered by this respondent;

- checking for missing values, where a question has not been answered when it should have been;

- checking for inconsistencies, where a respondent has contradicted him- or herself at different questions;

- outlying values, where a numerical answer has been given that is suspiciously different from other answers or not possible (for instance, the number of pizzas eaten per week by a person is given as 200).

With CAPI, CATI and CAWI surveys, some of these steps will be carried out automatically.

The final stage in data processing may be to apply *weighting* to the data. As we saw in Chapter 5, it is important that a sample in a quantitative study is representative of the population of interest. Each separate group within the sample should be represented in proportion to its presence in the population as a whole. For example, if health-food manufacturer HealthTreats is researching customer satisfaction and knows that 35 per cent of its customers are women aged 25–40, we would expect this group to make up 35 per cent of the sample. However, in some cases it may not be possible to sample in proportion to presence in the population. HealthTreats' sample might only have included 20 per cent women in the target age group, meaning that these women were under-represented in the sample. To compensate for this, the data can be weighted, with results for this group being scaled up in order to represent this target group in its true proportion within the population. Weighting can also be used to scale down results from groups that were over-represented in the original sample.

Analysing quantitative data

With the responses to the pre-coded and the open-ended questions entered on to the computer, data tables can be run.

Creating data tables

Data tables count the number of people who gave each response to a particular question. These counts can be expressed as percentages of the total sample or of a subgroup of the sample.

Table 9.1 shows the results for a question taken from HealthTreats' survey. At the left-hand side, the total percentages are given for each answer. However, the table also provides a breakdown of the answers given by different groups within the sample. This form of table is a ***cross-tabulation*** where responses are shown for a series of sub-groups, such as age or gender, or by responses to another question.

Table 9.1   *A cross-tabulation*
How often do you buy HealthTreats products?

	Total	Men under 25	Women under 25	Men 25–40	Women 25–40	Men 41+	Women 41+
Sample size	600	90	85	115	90	95	110
At least once a week	32%	18%	29%	32%	39%	26%	34%
At least once a month	41%	33%	38%	37%	48%	42%	51%
Less than once per month	27%	49%	33%	31%	13%	32%	15%

It is important to identify which cross-tabulations are needed when specifying the data analysis. The company may wish to find out about the responses of all the various age groups for each question. However, it might also need to compare answers given for two different questions. Using a cross-tabulation, it could, for example, examine the data to find out if people who buy HealthTreats' products frequently also buy vitamin supplements.

Identifying types of data

When analysing the responses to each question, it's vital to be aware of the types of data that you are dealing with. The client needs to know how the results can be interpreted. Different types of data can lead to different levels of analysis and interpretation. There are four principal types of data:

■ nominal;

■ ordinal;

■ interval;

■ ratio.

Nominal data

Nominal data is data that is categorized by name. For example, in the following question, the number 1 represents the answer 'male' and the number 2 represents 'female'.

Are you male or female?   Male [1]   Female [2]

The numbers are not being used as mathematical figures, merely as symbols to represent the responses, and could just as easily be the other way round. Using numeric codes such as these to represent answers makes the task of entering and analysing the data easier and more efficient. However, the data cannot be used to identify relationships between respondents' views. We only know that a certain number of respondents chose (1) and others chose (2).

Ordinal data

Unlike nominal data, the numbers in ordinal data have meaning. Look at the question below:

What features do you look for in a gym? Indicate order of importance from 1 to 5, where 1 = most important and 5 = least important.

■   large gym area

■   modern gym equipment

■   swimming pool

■   wide range of exercise classes

■   relaxation area.

In this question, the sequence of the numbers has meaning. The high code (1) indicates high importance, down to 5 (least important). In ordinal data, therefore, the position of one code relative to another is informative – the codes indicate the order in which the respondent views the options. If a gym is considering making improvements, it is likely to be looking at the higher codes to find out what customers appreciate most. However, if it needs to cut back on the facilities it provides, it needs to look at the lower codes in order to see what matters least to customers.

Interval data

Interval scales rate each item on a scale. The points on the scale are the same distance apart, but there is no mathematical link between the points. Table 9.2 gives an example.

In this question, we know that Respondent A who rates the exercise classes as (4) likes them more than Respondent B who rates them as (2). However, we can't say that Respondent A likes them twice as much as Respondent B. Interval scales simply indicate points along a scale. They do not show how these points relate to each other.

Table 9.2 *Sample of interval scale*
How do you rate the following facilities at your gym?
Please give a rating of 1 to 5 where 1 equals poor and 5 equals excellent

Facilities	5	4	3	2	1
Gym equipment					
Exercise classes					
Changing rooms					

Ratio data

Unlike interval data, ratio data does show the relationship between points on a scale.

How many times have you visited the gym in the past 7 days?

1. Five or more times

2. Four times

3. Three times

4. Twice

5. Once

6. I haven't been to the gym during the past 7 days.

In this example, we can see that a respondent who chooses (2) has been to the gym twice as often as one who chooses (4). Like interval data, therefore, ratio data can show how respondents' answers compare statistically with each other. Ratio data can also provide more insight into how these responses perform in relation to each other.

Being able to identify the type of data a question will produce is important. If the client wants to see how certain aspects of a product or brand perform in relation to each other, or to understand the range of attitudes expressed by consumers, interval and ratio data will provide this type of information. However, if it simply needs to know the order of preference for a set of items, or whether customers have bought a particular product, ordinal and nominal data will be required.

Data types: practice task

Look at the following questions. For each one, identify the type of data being collected.

1. Where did you go for your main holiday last year?

2. Which of the brands on this card have you heard of?
   - L'Oreal
   - Green People
   - Garnier
   - Wella
   - Aveda

3. Please put these five cars in the order in which you would prefer to own them.
   - Volkswagen Polo
   - Citroen C3
   - Toyota Yaris
   - Mini Cooper
   - Smart Car

4. What proportion of your household income do you spend on food each week?

5. On a scale from 1 to 10, where 1 is very dissatisfied and 10 very satisfied, how satisfied were you with the service you received today?

Compare your answers on page 145.

Identifying average scores

Identifying an average score can be useful in helping a client understand how well or badly its product or brand is performing. For example, if the gym owners know that the average score for their changing facilities is between 1 and 2 out of 5, they know that this is an area customers are not very satisfied with.

Average scores can be calculated on all data except nominal data. This calculation is done by allocating an arithmetical score to each possible response. A typical scoring system for an interval data agree-disagree scale for attitude statements might be:

Agree strongly:	+2
Agree slightly:	+1
Neither agree nor disagree:	0
Disagree slightly:	−1
Disagree strongly:	−2

A positive average – or *mean* – score indicates overall agreement with the statement, and a negative mean score indicates disagreement. You can look at different sub-groups to see if one group agrees more strongly than another group.

Taking analysis a step further

There are a range of multivariate analysis techniques that can be used for more sophisticated analyses. These techniques allow variables to be compared in a wide variety of ways. Some of the most commonly used multivariate techniques include:

- **Correlation analysis** tests the strength of a relationship between two sets of data, such as answers to two questions.
- **Regression analysis** is used to predict the answer to one question from answers to others.
- **Factor analysis** groups different questions by how similarly they are answered.
- **Cluster analysis** groups respondents according to how similarly they answer questions.

Multivariate analysis needs responses from different questions to be drawn together in different ways. As a result, it is important to specify at the questionnaire design stage that multivariate analysis is required. This will ensure that appropriate questions are asked and responses recorded in an appropriate way.

Interpreting the data

Once the analysis has been completed and the data tables produced, the researcher has to work out what the data means. Interpreting the data means identifying the key findings and understanding what they mean in relation to the research objectives. There are usually three stages in the interpretation process for the researcher:

- confirm;
- explore;
- refine and reduce.

Stage 1: Confirm

'Confirming' means satisfying yourself that the data you have is correct and complete. Errors might have occurred in any of the data collection, entry and analysis processes and, despite all safeguards taken, it is possible that some will be undetected. Questions that need to be asked at this stage include:

- Is this the most up-to-date set of data and has it been fully edited and corrected?
- Does the data set include data for all of the questions asked?
- Is the number of respondents as expected?
- If the data has been weighted, has the weighting worked as it should have done?

- Does the data at each question make sense?

- Does the data appear contradictory between questions?

- Is there a high proportion of 'not answered' or 'don't know' responses?

Having a 'common sense' check of the data is very important. Findings that seems surprising could indicate errors in the processing of the data.

Stage 2: Explore

At this stage, the aim is to look at the data for the story that is coming out. You may have seen patterns in the data at the 'confirm' stage, but now you need to see how the data fits together and answers the objectives. To do this, you need to do the following.

Revisit the objectives

When interpreting the data, it is important to remember why it was collected in the first place. Go back to the objectives of the survey and organize the data against those objectives. Then examine the data that is relevant to each objective in turn. Don't forget that the answers to one question may be relevant to more than one objective.

For each objective look for the main overall finding first – how many people like the concept; which one is preferred; whether more people claim to use Brand A than Brand B, and so on. Look for support for the finding from other questions, and if they appear to be contradictory ask yourself why.

It is important in understanding the data to remember the exact wording of the question asked. If you are not familiar with the question wording you can draw the wrong conclusion from the data. Differences in question wording between two questions on the same topic can lead to apparently contradictory answers.

Identify patterns

The analysis will have produced the cross-tabulations that were requested. Look at the data by subgroups to see if there are any patterns. Is there a difference between age groups in which product is preferred? Do people who buy a lot of a particular type of product prefer one brand to another? This type of analysis might suggest that different subgroups behave or think differently.

There might also be different groupings that can be spotted within the answers. With numeric data, an average score can hide the fact that a large minority of respondents gave a low amount as their answer, and another large minority gave a very high amount. It is possible that no one actually gave the average amount as the answer. This can be important as it indicates that there are two distinct groups in the research population.

Use appropriate statistical tests

All surveys are subject to *sampling error*. This can occur if the sample that was used was not perfectly representative of the population of interest. If a random sampling method is used then it is possible to calculate the sampling error for any given sample size. Generally, the bigger the sample size, the smaller the sampling error.

The aim of the quantitative survey is to be able to generalize findings to the population of interest as a whole. However, we need to take into account the possible sampling error. To do this, we can calculate the *confidence interval*. The confidence interval shows how sure we can be of the results, when sampling error is taken into account. This can be calculated for different levels of certainty, although 95 per cent is most commonly used. This means that there is 1 chance in 20 (5 per cent) that the real answer in the population lies outside of this range.

We can also calculate whether there is a significant difference between two figures from different samples or subsamples. Where two figures are not significantly different from each other, we need to be cautious about saying that they are different. There is a reasonable probability that the difference has arisen by chance.

These *significance tests* should be carried out by someone who has some training in statistics.

Stage 3: Refine and reduce

Once data and evidence has been accumulated to address the objectives, the next stage is to refine and reduce it to the key findings and any recommendations that should be made. At this stage, you bring together data from different questions to provide evidence to support the conclusions succinctly. You might not need to use all of the data that has been collected. However, you need to be sure that the data you don't use either supports your conclusion or does not contradict it. You cannot ignore and leave out data because it is contradictory. Any contradictions must be explained.

You may introduce background data from secondary research at this stage, in order to supply further evidence to support your conclusions, or to expose apparent contradictions.

Investigating the figures: practice task

In the UK, the National Statistics website provides access to all data gathered during the national census. This makes an excellent resource if you want to look at data sets in more detail.

You can download statistics on a wide range of topics. If you live in the UK, why not try to find out more about your local area by downloading and reviewing sets of data?

Visit www.statistics.gov.uk or www.neighbourhood.statistics.gov.uk

Analysing qualitative data

As we saw in Chapter 7, data from qualitative research techniques is frequently collected using voice or video recordings, or occasionally from notes made of the group discussions or depth interviews. In order to begin the analysis process, it is important to transcribe any recordings so that you can see the exact data you have to work on.

Although the type of data that has been collected is very different from that in quantitative studies, many of the principles of effective analysis remain the same.

Check the data is correct

As with quantitative data, the first step is to confirm that the data is what it ought to be. To do this, the questions that need to be asked are:

▨ **Was the sample recruited correctly?** If it wasn't recruited to the original specification, was that because it was deliberately changed, or was it an error?

▨ **Was there any bias in the sample?** You need to take this into account when you are assessing the information.

▨ **Were there any environmental factors that might have affected responses?** Issues such as the location, external noise or the temperature in the venue might have affected the way respondents took part in the research.

Return to the research objectives

Both quantitative and qualitative research are undertaken to address specific objectives. The next step, therefore, is to think about the data in relation to the research objectives:

▨ Do you have enough information to give a satisfactory answer to the problem?

▨ Does a re-reading of the brief and the proposal reveal any further understanding of the background to the business problem? This can help to give meaning to the data.

Organize the data

Just as quantitative data needs to be organized and grouped, so too does qualitative data. It is important to identify how the data needs to be grouped for analysis. For example, research is often designed to uncover the views of different subgroups in the population, such as age groups, gender or product usage groups. It is important, therefore, to keep the responses from the different groups of interest separate in order to determine the major similarities and differences between them. However, it is also important to gain an overview of the sample's views in relation to the different topics included in the research objectives.

With quantitative data, the process of coding into a computer program allows manipulation of the data. However, with qualitative data, the early stages of analysis may require multiple copies of transcripts to be made and stored in different ways. For example, the data from the different groups needs to be filed separately. This can be done by organizing it in a matrix, by colour coding the transcripts, or by holding electronic copies of the transcripts in different files or folders on the computer.

However it is stored, it is important that the data is organized so that it can be easily scanned and read across the sample, and that similarities and differences both within and between groups can be identified easily.

Coding the data

Aggregating verbal (as opposed to numeric) data is a complex task. However, just as quantitative data is coded for ease of analysis, it is also possible to create a codified approach to qualitative data.

Codifying qualitative data

In an exploratory study of shampoo, a female respondent said:

> I buy the one for the family. I get the green one – I forget the name. It's got a conditioner in it which is good for me because I have long hair. But it's not too thick for my husband. He sometimes gets dandruff.

When analysing this statement, the researcher identified a number of discrete points:

- Woman buys for family.
- Recognition of brand by colour.
- Has conditioner in it.
- Conditioner linked to long hair.
- Conditioner = thick texture?
- Dandruff associated with non-creamy shampoos?

The points are given 'facts' as reported by the consumer. By giving each of these points a code, the researcher can identify them if these or similar points arise later in the data. This process allows the key points to emerge from the data, and similarities and differences to be identified more easily.

When all topics have been allocated a code, then the second stage of coding takes place. This is to read across the matrix looking for areas of similarity and difference between the groups. Do the same points recur across all groups in the study? By reading across the groups and within the groups, it is possible to build a picture of the prevalent views expressed by the respondents. This process gives some idea of who said what, and how it was said.

Analyse the data

With the data drawn together, you can begin the real search for meaning in it. The focus of this analysis will be determined largely by the objectives of the study, and you must revisit these in order to set yourself the right questions to answer. For example, if the aim of the study was to find out the most appropriate way for a new clothing company to communicate with its target audience, then it might be important to look at what the data tells you about:

■ the factors that influence decision making when buying clothes;

■ where the target consumers get their information about fashion;

■ what role the media play in the market the company wants to enter;

■ which media reach the target consumers and carry the right message.

The process of coding might have allowed a range of views on each of these areas to emerge across the groups of respondents. The researcher's role is to identify which are the most common, which contrast with each other, and whether any points contradict the prevalent views expressed by the majority of respondents. It is important to remember that, in qualitative research, the focus of analysis needs to be on what was said, not simply the number of people who expressed the view.

Getting the most from the questionnaire: case study

The data collection for the quantitative stage of the research for T H Stores has now been completed. The research consultant now has 150 completed questionnaires. However, one of the owners who has become interested in research is very anxious to have the results. He does not understand why he cannot simply read through the completed questionnaires in order to understand what the customers want.

What are the key issues which the owner needs to understand about:

■ data processing?

■ analysing data?

Make notes on the issues, then check your answers by reviewing the sections on data processing and quantitative analysis.

Terminology test

The following research terms were introduced in this chapter. Can you explain what each one means?

- code frame
- data entry
- weighting
- mean
- confidence interval

- data processing
- data editing
- cross-tabulation
- sampling error
- significance test

Summary

Analysis of quantitative data requires a number of steps in order to put the data into a form that can be analysed and then to interpret it. Don't forget to:

- Code all the questions on the questionnaire. You may need to devise a code frame for open-ended questions.
- Edit the data for errors and inconsistencies.
- Produce data tables that address the questions asked in the research objectives.
- Identify the type of data you are working with. Different types of data can be analysed in different ways.
- Carry out a 'common sense' check on all data and data tables. Can you explain any unusual patterns or findings?

Qualitative analysis has the same eventual objective, but is a more flexible process. Always remember to:

- Transcribe the audio or video tapes.
- Confirm that you have enough data, and that it addresses the needs of the research objectives.
- Organize, store and code the data by relevant subgroups.
- Look for areas of difference or similarity between subgroups.
- Analyse the data against the research questions in order to meet the objectives.

10

What do I do with the information?

Reporting and communicating research findings

Introduction

When all of the data has been analysed and interpreted, it is time to report the findings to the client. It is important to remember that the research has been carried out to help solve a problem or make a decision. Good reporting can help turn research findings into action.

In this chapter, you will learn how to:

■ identify how research findings can really help the client;

■ select the best approach to delivering the information to the client;

■ help the client make sense of the information;

■ structure an effective research report;

■ present the information in a way which adds value for the client.

Identifying the links between the findings and the problem

In Chapter 2, we looked at the importance of exploring the business problem before beginning the research process. As the research project develops, it is vital to bear in mind the research objectives, and why the information is needed. And once all of the data has been analysed, it is time to return to the original problem and find out how the findings relate to it. When clients commission research, they are looking for evidence to help them make a decision. The role of the researcher, in reporting the findings, is to help show how the evidence from the research findings can be used in the decision-making process. However, don't forget that it is the client's responsibility to take the business decision, with the researcher acting as an advisor on the strengths – and limitations – of the evidence.

In order to give useful and accurate advice, there are a number of questions you need to consider:

■ **How do the research objectives relate to the business problem?** In Chapter 2, we looked at the business problem facing T H Stores. Its owners wanted to decide on the best way to expand their business. However, the research project that developed focused on one possible area of expansion: what would encourage customers to shop at an enlarged T H Stores shop? This project did not look at any other possible ways of expansion, and so only provides part of the evidence if the owners are trying to decide between expanding this store and opening a new store. It is important to remember that the research objectives may relate to only part of the possible business decision.

■ **What are the strengths – and limitations – of the research methodology?** We have seen that the research objectives may only address part of the business problem, but the chosen methods too might only be able to provide a partial picture of the situation. For example, the qualitative study into possible names for an aftershave which was discussed in Chapter 7 could provide some ideas for names for the product. However, it would not provide information on how popular the various suggestions might be among the population as a whole. It is important to identify what the evidence does – and doesn't – provide in relation to the business problem.

■ **How valid and reliable is the information?** In Chapters 5, 6 and 9, we looked at the importance of validity and reliability in collecting quantitative data. The make-up of the sample, the number of respondents and the way in which the data is processed and analysed can all have an important impact on the strength and accuracy of information. In planning how to report the information, it is important to consider what the findings really tell you about the range and strength of respondents' views. The researcher must be able to tell the client how accurate, valid and reliable the findings are.

■ **Are the findings what you expected, or are there surprises?** During the research project, the researcher may develop a 'feel' for the findings. As the data is processed and at the beginning of analysis, some clear and expected patterns may start to emerge. However, it is possible that some findings will come as a surprise. For example, the research into the possible expansion of T H Stores focused on the best way to expand the store. However, analysis of the data might show that the majority of customers don't want a larger shop – they are happy with the shop as it is. The researcher needs to identify any issues that appear to contradict expected patterns, and to consider how these affect the way the research can inform the business decision.

Once you have developed a clear and comprehensive understanding of how the research findings address the research objectives and the business problem, it is time to consider how this can be conveyed to the client. Most clients will expect a written report which gives detailed information about the findings. They might also want the information to be delivered in a number of ways, must usually through a face-to-face or video presentation. However, it is important to note that the team members giving the presentation might not be those who were most closely involved in collecting and analysing the data. When choosing the approach to reporting findings, therefore, there are some key issues to consider.

Selecting the best approach to delivering findings

The checklist below will help you decide how to choose the most appropriate approach.

1. **Check the agreed proposal.** Remember that the proposal normally contains a section on 'deliverables', or what should be delivered to the client at the end of the project. This will normally stipulate how the information will be shared, including how it should be presented and the number of copies or presentations which need to be provided. Don't forget, however, that some changes may have been discussed as the project progressed. It is important to make sure that the deliverables list you are working to is the one that has been agreed with the client.

2. **Consider what the client wants to do with the information.** Just as researchers differ in the ways they approach research problems, so clients differ in the way they use research information. Some may want to understand the findings in detail, then use the information to make their own decisions. Others may need help in making links between the findings and any action they can take. Knowing how the client wants to use the information will help you adapt the focus of your written report or presentation to the individual client.

3. **Find out about the audience.** Who makes up the audience for your report or presentation? It might be that you have several different audiences. For example, a bank that has commissioned research into the best way to encourage young people to save money might need the information for its internal marketing team. However, senior directors in other departments might need to understand how the research could impact on their departments.

As a result, it might be necessary to present or report on the findings in different formats, with headline information and recommendations for the senior directors and more in-depth information for the marketing department. Remember, it is vital to tailor your approach to meet the needs of different audiences.

4. **Check with your client contact.** It is important to remember that you may have been working with a contact person in the client company, and that your contact can help you identify priorities for the report or presentation. Gaining an inside view of your audience from your contact can help you decide how to handle information and potential questions. This is particularly useful if the research has uncovered sensitive issues or 'bad news' for the client.

Preparing to communicate research findings: practice task

A&L Santese is an Italian retail company which specializes in designer clothing. With a chain of designer stores around Italy, the owners are now interested in setting up a branch in the UK. They commissioned research from a UK-based research agency to find out how viable and profitable this move would be. The agency is now preparing to report its findings.

What issues do the agency need to consider to make sure that the company can make good use of the findings? Make a note of your ideas, then compare your answer with the suggestion on page 146. Remember that there might be a range of issues which you need to consider.

Helping the client to make sense of the findings

Once the researcher has identified the information that needs to be included in any report, and the best overall approach to take, it is time to begin work on the report and/or presentation. The key to an effective report is to ensure that the results can be easily understood by the client's staff, even though they have not been involved in carrying out the project. A large amount of data might have been collected during the project, but you may have only 30 minutes to help the client understand its importance. There are a number of steps the researcher can take to make sure that the client understands the importance and relevance of the research findings.

Making numbers easy to follow

Quantitative studies produce results in the form of lists of numbers and statistics. The first step in making the findings clear is to find a way to help the client make sense of these numbers quickly. Here are some of the most common techniques used to help clients see numbers easily.

■ **Rounding numbers up or down.** The analysis of quantitative data can result in complex statistics. For example, you might find that 36.564 per cent of the sample of 2,045 respondents agreed with a particular statement. However, if all results are expressed in percentages to three decimal points, it can be difficult for the client to follow the numbers. By rounding the number up to one decimal point (36.6 per cent) or even to the next whole number (37 per cent), it is easier to understand what this means in real terms. Rounding numbers can help make the results accessible very quickly. However, it is important to remember that rounding does make results less accurate. When we say that 37 per cent – rather than 36.564 per cent – of people agreed, we are making a change to the result of 0.436 per cent. How numbers are rounded, therefore, depends on the level of accuracy the client expects to be shown in the results.

■ **Creating clear tables.** One of the most common ways to present quantitative data is in a table. They can help the client to quickly understand the key results. However, a poorly organized table can be confusing. To make tables easy to read, always:
   – Make sure each column and row is clearly labelled so the client can see at a glance what each figure relates to.
   – Have a clear organizing principle for the rows and for the columns. For example, a shoe company might want to know about any changes in the types of customers buying its shoes over a five-year period. In a table showing these results, each column could show results for a different year, with each row being a different type of customer. To help the client see the changes clearly, you need to decide how to organize the customer rows. Will you put the largest or smallest group of current customers at the top? Or will you organize the data according to the largest or smallest groups when the study began five years ago? Numbers organized in ascending or descending order are easier to understand than those that are not.

■ **Using graphs and charts.** Visual representation of numbers through graphs and charts can make results immediately accessible. However, there are some golden rules governing how you use these visual aids. Make sure you:
   – Label each element of the graph or chart clearly to show what each represents. For example, if you are using a bar chart, such as the one in Figure 10.1, you need to make sure you label each axis as well as each of the bars. This ensures that the client can understand immediately the relevance of each item in the graph or chart.
   – Show how the numbers progress. Clients need to see at a glance how each group of customers compares with the others.

■ The most important point to bear in mind is that figures should always give clear and accurate information, and should never mislead the client. When using tables and graphs to represent responses by the sample, it's vital to indicate clearly the size of the sample.

Identifying key findings

In addition to making the actual figures transparent, it's important to consider which findings are key for the client to understand. The researcher needs to identify which information is vital, and which is simply interesting. To do this, try to:

■ **Identify patterns in the information.** Whether the information being reported on is qualitative or quantitative, you need to be able to identify key themes or trends. In particular, being able to make links between findings in one part of the research and those in other parts will help the client to see how the whole picture fits together.

■ **How real or significant are the differences you have identified?** In Chapter 9, we looked at the importance of working out whether differences identified in quantitative data are statistically significant. For example, Figure 10.1 shows that slightly more of the shoe company's male customers aged 55–64 buy more than one pair of shoes per year than those in the 45–54 age group. However, given that the overall percentage of customers in these groups buying more than one pair of shoes is fairly small, it is possible that this difference is not terribly important. Try to ensure that you identify the differences that are of real importance to the client.

■ **What's normal?** The figure also shows that the percentage of women in the 65+ age group who buy more than one pair of shoes per year is far below that for women in the other age groups. How worried should the company be about this apparent difference? It is important to be able to provide wider contextual information for comparison. For example, other research studies might show that it is usual for women in this age group to buy fewer items of clothing, possibly because they are likely to have a

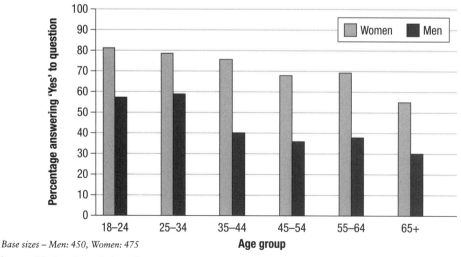

Base sizes – Men: 450, Women: 475

Figure 10.1 *Sample bar chart*

smaller income. Providing a way of helping clients to create a benchmark for what is normal, or what they should expect, can help put findings in perspective.

When preparing to report back on research findings, it is vital to look at issues from the client's perspective. What do people really need to know? How can the information be made as clear as possible? Many clients will have only a limited time to spend on listening to or reading the results of the research. You need to consider how to help them make the best use of that time.

Organizing information for maximum impact: practice task

For a number of years, a local council has carried out an annual survey into levels of participation in organized sport by schoolchildren in local secondary schools. Table 10.1 shows the results for one of the questions in the survey over a two-year period.

Table 10.1 *Sample table*
Which of the following sports do you play regularly (ie once per month or more)?
(G = Girls; B = Boys)

	Year 1	Year 2	Year-on-year change
Athletics	24.6% (G); 31% (B)	25.25%(G); 29.2%(B)	+6.25%(G); –1.8%(B)
Tennis	8% (G); 7.9%(B)	8.01%(G); 7.7% (B)	+0.01%(G); –0.2%(B)
Football	2%(G); 57.1%(B)	3.1%(G); 63.1%(B)	+1.1%(G); +4%(B)
Rugby	0%(G); 21.34%(B)	0.1%(G); 19.5%(B)	+0.1%(G); –1.84%(B)
Basketball	4.67%(G); 17%(B)	4.76%(G); 19.1%(B)	+0.09%(G); +2.1%(B)

There are some problems with this table. Identify three things you could do to make it easier to read and understand the results. Make notes about your ideas, then compare them with those on page 146.

Structuring an effective research report

Clients usually need a written report on the research they have commissioned, providing information about how the research was carried out and what was discovered. However, the report needs to strike a balance between giving full and accurate information and being useful for the client. It is important to keep in mind the issue of usefulness – it will help you to structure the report and highlight the key issues.

Although research agencies may have their own, in-house style for reports, most research reports follow a similar structure. The sections include:

▪ **A title page.** If the report is going to be filed, it needs to be easy to retrieve. An easily recognizable title page can help clients access the report when they need to.

▪ **An informative contents page.** Make sure the information is easy to find by providing guidance on all the main sections, including the appendices, in the contents page.

▪ **An executive summary.** An executive summary is a short overview of the research: why it was carried out, what was done, the key findings and any recommendations. A good two-page summary will help busy clients identify immediately what needs to be learnt from the research. In some cases, clients even specify that the summary must never be more than one page long.

▪ **Introduction.** This section should describe the context for the research. It demonstrates how fully the researcher has understood the client's business context, and the importance of the business problem. It also needs to identify why research was necessary.

▪ **Research objectives.** Highlighting the objectives will show exactly what the research was designed to achieve.

▪ **Research methods.** A brief description of how the research was carried out, including the sample, data collection and analysis methods, is what is required here. But keep this section sharp and focused – the client needs to know what was done, but does not necessarily want to be drowned in technical detail.

▪ **Findings.** What are the main findings and how do these relate to the research objectives? What should the client learn from this research project? Think carefully about the key issues that have emerged and how these relate to the original problem. Don't forget that you need to be able to support each finding with evidence from the data. Use this section to draw out key areas, and provide the supporting evidence in the appendices.

▪ **Summary and recommendations.** What can you say in conclusion about the research problem, based on the research you have discussed? What might the next steps be for the client? Being able to highlight possible next steps can provide the help the client needs to take action, based on the research.

▪ **Appendices.** Although the client may not need detailed information in the body of the report, the appendices should allow people to explore the research further if they want to. You need to include all the details of each step of the process, including information about the sampling, copies of questionnaires or topic guides, information about how the data was analysed, and all data tables. Remember to label each appendix clearly and list each in the contents page.

Writing the report: mind your language!

It is important to remember that the report is a formal business document, which may be circulated by the client. As a result, the tone and presentation of the report need to be appropriate to a professional document. Don't forget to check and recheck the document as you write it. Is it clearly structured and signposted? Is it easy to read? Are there any grammatical or spelling errors that need to be corrected? If you are unsure, ask a colleague to read it for you and give you a second opinion.

Adding value with your presentation

In addition to the written report, many clients ask the researcher to present the results of the project. The presentation needs to help the client do two things: understand the implications of the research for the business problem, and identify how the research evidence can help solve the problem. So how can the researcher present the research information in a way that meets the client's needs? Here are some dos and don'ts for creating a good presentation.

Do

■ **Find out who is coming to the presentation, and their interest in the project.** Researchers often find that, within the client organization, there are differing views about the usefulness of this research. Knowing who will be in the audience, their role in the organization, and how they view this project can help the researcher tailor the presentation for maximum effect.

■ **Identify the 'story' the research tells.** The presentation needs to provide information that is memorable and useful. To help the client make the most of the presentation, try to think of it as a story: the story begins with the need to find an answer to a problem. How do the findings help resolve that problem?

■ **Fine-tune your presentation skills.** Being able to engage the audience means understanding how they feel, what they need to know, and how they can leave feeling that the presentation was worthwhile. Practising the presentation with someone who will give constructive criticism and ask 'difficult' questions can help the researcher to deal with any tricky issues the client might raise.

■ **Provide an opportunity for questions and follow-up.** The aim of the presentation is to enable clients to see how they can use the information to solve their problem. The researcher can really add value by showing the client the possible ways forward: if you were in the client's shoes, what would you do next, based on the research evidence? Being able to provide the client with possible solutions based on the evidence can really help turn the findings into action.

■ **Follow up the presentation with a discussion of future action.** Many projects are commissioned but never acted upon. In some cases, this is because the research findings did not support the direction the client wished to take. However, in other cases, the client needs help in making best use of the findings. It is always a good idea to follow up a presentation with a further call or meeting to discuss the range of ways in which the research might help the organization.

Don't

■ **Drown the client in detail.** Clients normally have only a short time to take on board the key issues identified by the research. They need to understand what was discovered, and what that means for the business problem. As a result, a long description of the technical aspects of the project is unlikely to be what is needed. The technical description needs to contain certain key facts such as sample size and be sufficient to convince the audience of the validity of the findings, but no longer than that. Keep the technical descriptions short to allow for more discussion of the findings. For more information on the detail that should be included, see the MRS Code of Conduct and the associated Reporting Guidelines. Both documents can be downloaded from the MRS website.

■ **Think of the presentation as a set of slides.** The majority of presentations include a range of visual slides, intended to help the audience understand and remember what has been said. However, it is very easy to fall into the trap of producing large numbers of slides which overwhelm the audience with information, or include too much animation which detracts from the message. Remember to think of the slides as a visual aid: what does each slide help the audience to do or understand? If you are not sure, don't include the slide in the presentation.

■ **Leave anything to chance.** The presentation may be held in the client's offices, in the research agency or in specially rented premises. Wherever it is being held, it is important to check practical details. How many people will there be in the room? What technical equipment is available (such as lap-tops and projectors)? What is the layout of the room? Being fully aware of all of the practical details can help make planning the presentation easier.

Remember, for many people in the audience the presentation is the main exposure they have to the survey and its results. Often it is the only exposure. This is your one chance to show them what a good job you have done. A good presentation reflects well on you, on the person at the client company who commissioned you, and on the status of research within the client organization.

Remember too that the researcher's relationship with the client need not end with the presentation. The findings of the research project might be useful in many ways for the client. For example, the qualitative research into the possibilities of launching a new format for the newspaper that we discussed in Chapter 3 might have uncovered lots of suggestions for features and developments. Being able to identify how the newspaper owners might use this information to best effect can make the researcher an invaluable support to the organization.

Finally, don't forget that the end of a project is an excellent opportunity for the researcher to reflect on what has been learnt during the process of research. This may include a review of the research choices along the way. Was the best data collection method chosen? What might have happened if the sample had been drawn in a different way? What has been learnt about the sector the client works in? Reviewing and reflecting on the strengths and weaknesses of the project will help researchers to develop their skills further.

Presenting the findings: case study

The study into the possibility of expanding T H Stores has been completed, and the research consultant is almost ready to deliver a presentation on the findings. Two days before the presentation, she has a meeting with her key contact to discuss what the client wants from the presentation.

Make a list of some of the questions the research consultant should ask her contact to ensure she is fully prepared for the presentation. Compare your list with our suggestions on page 147. Remember that all suggestions are simply guidelines – there are no completely right or wrong answers.

Summary

Reporting on findings brings the research process to a close, but it is probably the most important step in that process. Remember:

■ The research was carried out to help solve a problem. It is vital to review the findings to see whether the evidence can do this.

■ The client is interested in the findings, rather than the technical detail of research. Make sure that any report helps the client make sense of the evidence.

■ Presenting findings gives the researcher the opportunity to show how the research might lead to action. Try to identify what action you would recommend, and why.

■ Take time to review what has been learnt from the research process. Reflection on the whole process can lead to improved performance next time round.

11

Where do I go from here?

Developing your career in market research

Introduction

In previous chapters, we have looked at the range of work undertaken in the market research sector, and at the roles of some of the people who carry out that work. As we have shown, different areas of research require very different types of skills. For example, those involved in data analysis need highly developed analytical and IT skills, while those involved in moderating discussion groups or carrying out depth interviews need to have excellent interpersonal skills. If you are interested in pursuing a career in market research, it's likely that there is a role that matches your skill set.

In this chapter, you will learn about:

- the professional associations that support the people who work in research;
- the career opportunities that exist in the research sector;
- steps you can take to develop your own research career.

Professional associations for the profession

What is the role of a professional body or professional association? In many cases, it helps raise and maintain professional standards, provides opportunities for professional development and provides a forum for the exchange of ideas and discussion of issues of concern to the profession. In the research sector in the UK, a range of professional bodies offers support and services for different segments of the research profession.

- **MRS (Market Research Society).** MRS is the largest of all the professional bodies serving the research community. As we saw in Chapter 1, MRS provides a regulatory framework for the conduct of market, social and opinion research. However, the organization is also very active in other areas, including organizing training programmes and conferences, publishing a range of magazines and journals, and supporting a range of network groups so that researchers with similar interests can meet together. In addition, MRS is the awarding body for a suite of professional qualifications for researchers. For more information about MRS membership and services, visit www.mrs.org.uk

- **SRA (Social Research Association).** The work of the SRA was also highlighted in Chapter 1. SRA has a role to play in advising on best practice standards in social research. Its *Ethical Guidelines* provide a framework for ethical good practice in social research projects. Like MRS, it offers advice on careers in research, as well as journals and newsletters and links to other social research organizations. Find out more at www.the-sra.org.uk

- **AQR (Association of Qualitative Researchers).** Like SRA, AQR has a role to play in advising on best practice, in this case on qualitative research. It aims to provide support for best practice through training and networking events, books and journals, and advice on working in qualitative research. If you are interested in qualitative research, visit the website at www.aqr.org.uk

- **ESOMAR.** Based in the Netherlands, ESOMAR is a European professional body. Like MRS, it publishes an ethical code, the *ESOMAR World Research Code and Guidelines*, which members must abide by. In common with the other professional bodies, it also offers access to training and advice about working in research. For more information on ESOMAR, visit www.esomar.org

All the professional bodies listed offer advice and guidance for researchers at all stages in their careers, with websites filled with useful information. In addition, many other countries have their own national associations which can be found via the Research Buyers Guide (RBG) website (www.rbg.org.uk). By becoming a member of a professional body, you can make contact with a wide range of practitioners, and demonstrate your commitment to high standards in research.

Career opportunities in research

The research profession provides opportunities for people from many different backgrounds. In addition to qualitative research, which attracts those interested in working with people, and quantitative research, which allows those more interested in numbers to develop their skills, the growth in international research has meant that people with language skills are very welcome within the sector. Working as a clientside researcher can help those with a business or marketing background to combine research with their other skills, while working in a research agency will allow them to work effectively with clients and learn new, specialized skills. Researchers in smaller agencies may find that they have the opportunity to see a project through all its stages of development, while those in larger agencies may find that they are working on extremely large, complex projects with some of the world's largest clients.

All this demonstrates the range of opportunity that a career in research can provide. However, despite this variety, there is a relatively standard career route within the research profession as a whole.

- **Stage 1: Research executive or operations staff.** Within the UK, research is a graduate-led industry, in which the majority of entrants will already have achieved a first degree. The posts in agencies normally open to graduates are either that of (trainee) research executive, working on the development of projects, or in the Operations Department, normally working on data. At this stage in your career, you can expect to receive a substantial amount of training and may be working towards a professional qualification.

- **Stage 2: Senior research executive or operations manager.** Careers tend to develop quickly within the research industry, and many people move on to their first post of responsibility within three to four years of entering. As a senior research executive, you would expect to be in charge of at least some aspects of research projects, while in the Operations Department you might be leading teams of data processors or interviewers.

- **Stage 3: Associate director or consultant.** Staying in an agency could lead to the level of associate director within five to six years. This is a position of considerable responsibility, and often entails managing the accounts of a number of clients.

This is a very general, linear description of how a career in a research agency might progress. However, careers are rarely completely linear, and there is a great deal of movement between the agency and client sectors. With each step, you add to your skill set and make yourself a more flexible, and therefore more valuable, researcher.

Getting started in market research

So if you are not already working in research, how do you join the profession?

■ The first place to start is with the professional bodies. Contact them directly for information on careers in research.

■ Many of the larger research agencies offer training programmes for graduates and new recruits, some of which are linked to professional qualifications. To find out more about the training and careers opportunities offered by research agencies, visit the RBG on www.rbg.org.uk. And don't forget that many agencies are global companies, with offices in many countries, so if you are outside the UK, the RBG can help you identify major research companies working in your area.

■ Visit www.research-live.com, the online version of *Research*, the magazine for the research industry in the UK. In addition to news and information on latest industry practice, the website features a large recruitment section. Both agencies and clients advertise here, so you can find out about the type of work offered on both sides of research.

The research profession provides opportunities for people from many different backgrounds. To find out what's available for you, tap into a wide range of information sources via the internet.

Web search: practical task

Try to find out as much as possible about the five largest research agencies included in the *Research Buyer's Guide* (www.rbg.org.uk).

■ What are their names?

■ How many countries does each operate in?

■ Find three of their major research specialisms.

■ What career opportunities does each offer?

Terminology test

No new terminology was introduced in this chapter. However, return to any chapter that you have found challenging and repeat the terminology test in that chapter.

Summary

- A range of professional bodies exists to provide support to those working in research-related roles.

- Both MRS and ESOMAR produce codes of conduct to govern the conduct of research carried out by their members.

- The majority of people joining a research agency as a research executive are expected to have a university-level qualification. However, there are other routes into the industry, particularly for those who work in the operations side of agencies.

- The research industry provides opportunities for people with very differing skills. To find an agency that carries out the type of work you are interested in, search the RBG.

Test yourself revision section

This section is designed to help you revise some of the key information contained in Chapters 1 to 11. It also helps you prepare for the examination of the MRS/City & Guilds Certificate in Market and Social Research.

The MRS/City & Guilds Certificate in Market and Social Research

Developed in partnership between the Market Research Society (MRS) and City & Guilds, this qualification provides an ideal introduction for those who need to be more informed about the role of effective research in business decision making.

MRS, drawing on its expertise as the world's largest international membership organization for professional researchers and others engaged or interested in market, social and opinion research, is responsible for the development and review of the syllabus for the qualification.

City & Guilds, the UK's leading provider of vocational qualifications, administers all aspects of assessment, and is responsible for certificating candidates' achievements.

The MRS/City & Guilds Certificate is accredited at Level 2 in the UK's National Qualifications Framework.

Preparing for the examination

The examination for this qualification comprises 40 multiple-choice questions. This section provides you with examples of the type of questions you can expect to find in the exam. Answers to the questions can be found on page 148.

For further information about the MRS/City & Guilds Certificate in Market and Social Research, visit the MRS website (www.mrs.org.uk/training) or the City & Guilds website (www.city-and-guilds.co.uk/documents/6726_SH.pdf).

Test questions

Choose ONE answer only for each of the following questions. Answers can be found on page 148.

1. A research problem can be broken down into
   A   research objectives
   B   schedules
   C   proposals
   D   timelines

2. History of the business and background to the problem are part of the
   A   contract
   B   schedule
   C   objectives
   D   research brief

3. A researcher carrying out secondary research might
   A   telephone consumers
   B   look at work done by others
   C   count the number of people visiting a location
   D   send out questionnaires to be completed by an entire population

4. A researcher carrying out qualitative research might
   A   ask open-ended questions
   B   ask only yes–no questions
   C   count the number of people visiting a location
   D   send out identical questionnaires to a large population

5. A national census is an example of
   A   causal research
   B   descriptive research
   C   exploratory research
   D   longitudinal research

6. Which of the following will contain a description of the research design, methods, deliverables and resources?
   A   brief
   B   objectives
   C   proposal
   D   schedule

7. One reason why questionnaires are used is
    A   to save interviewers' time
    B   because participants are likely to complete them
    C   to ensure the same questions are asked every time
    D   because they give richer information than face-to-face interviews

8. How are answers to open-ended questions recorded on a questionnaire?:
    A   using dichotomous responses
    B   using pre-coded responses
    C   using rating scales
    D   verbatim

9. Depth interviews are especially useful when
    A   the subject matter is sensitive
    B   many people have to be asked the same questions
    C   results need to be produced very quickly
    D   the research budget is low

10. A sample frame is
    A   a list of those the researcher wants to concentrate on
    B   used to decide which sector to concentrate research on
    C   designed by the client to show their needs
    D   a list of all members of a population

11. Random sampling
    A   gives everyone in the population of interest the same chance of being selected
    B   gives the researcher the opportunity to focus on a smaller population of interest than usual
    C   is not a valid way of sampling for large-scale projects
    D   is usually used when time is limited

12. Which of the following is NOT a disadvantage of face-to-face interviewing?
    A   it is resource-intensive
    B   interviewers are highly skilled
    C   it can be difficult to identify participants
    D   proposed participants may be reluctant to take part

13. A company which wants to carry out a small amount of research and has a limited budget may use
    A   face-to-face interviews
    B   an omnibus survey
    C   hall tests
    D   CATI

14. Which of the following is not an example of qualitative data collection methods?
    A   depth interviews
    B   discussion groups
    C   structured questionnaire
    D   observation

15. An interviewer in qualitative research would probably
    A   conduct in-street interviews
    B   play little or no part in developing questions
    C   record answers using CAPI equipment
    D   record interviews using audio or video equipment

16. When potential participants are approached to take part in a survey, they should be told a number of things. Which of the following need they NOT be told?
    A   the name of the client
    B   the name of the company carrying out the research
    C   the approximate length of time the interview will take
    D   a broad indication of the subject matter of the survey

17. Social desirability bias occurs when
    A   respondents are chosen according to their demographic profile
    B   answers from unsuitable respondents are ignored
    C   there is a mismatch between interviewer and respondent
    D   respondents answer questions as they think they should, rather than honestly

18. Attitudinal rating scales are an example of
    A   nominal data
    B   ordinal data
    C   interval data
    D   ratio data

19. Ranking scales are an example of
    A   nominal data
    B   ordinal data
    C   interval data
    D   ratio data

20. Which of the following is NOT a membership organization for researchers?
    A   MRS
    B   SRA
    C   RBG
    D   AQR

Task answer guide

Chapter 2: Research objectives

Creating a research brief

Here are some suggestions for the background information which could be included in each brief:

The owner of a small restaurant wants to start selling her own brand of homemade sauces in specialist food shops:

▪ Information about the sauces: What kind of sauces? Which are most popular in the restaurant? Do clients ask to buy them? Are they sold to take away?

▪ Information about competitors: Who are the biggest competitors? How do the sauces differ from the competitors'?

▪ Information about specialist food shops: Which types of food shops (eg food from any particular area)? Have there been any enquiries from food shops about the sauces?

A local council wants residents to recycle more of their household waste:

▪ Information about current recycling: What, if anything, is currently recycled? What does the council do currently to encourage recycling?

▪ Information about items to be recycled: What would the council like to be recycled (eg paper, plastics, garden waste)?

▪ Information about other recycling schemes: What do neighbouring councils do?

An electronics company wants to move into a new overseas market:

▪ Information about the company, and its current market.

▪ Information about the possible target countries, and why they have been chosen.

■ Information about competitors' overseas markets.

Chapter 3: Research design

Primary or secondary, practice task

1. Secondary

2. Primary

3. Primary

4. Secondary

5. Primary

6. Primary

Quantitative or qualitative information, practice task

1. (Who are the customers?) Quantitative information – using a questionnaire to count the number of customers in an age group, and in different streets.

2. (Why do customers choose to shop here?) Probably qualitative – the owners don't necessarily know what draws in their customers. Questions that allow them to express their own ideas might identify a wide range of motivations.

3. (What range of goods do they buy here?) Quantitative – this information could be found, for example, by looking at the store's sales records.

4. (Where else do they shop, and why?) Probably both quantitative and qualitative. There is probably a restricted number of alternative shopping places, and you need to find out which one is the major competitor. To do this, you need to count the number of customers who shop at each different place. However, they may have lots of different reasons for shopping there. You might be able to guess at some (eg the other place is cheaper) but the shoppers need to be able to tell you others that are not so obvious.

5. (Would an enlarged shop encourage them to spend more here?) Probably qualitative. The owners need to understand what will motivate people most to spend more money with them. If you ask a yes/no question (eg Would you shop more here if the store was bigger?) you might not give the shoppers the opportunity to really think about their feelings about a bigger shop.

Exploring, describing or testing links

1. A *descriptive* research design is needed. The college principal needs to know what different colleges currently offer.

2. A *causal* research design is needed. The research project needs to test whether different types of gym users – those in exercise classes and those in one-to-one classes – lose weight more quickly than people who do not do these activities. They can then compare results for each type of gym user.

3. A *descriptive* research design is needed. The council needs a clear picture of crime in its area to compare with the national statistics.

4. An *exploratory* design is needed. The company does not know if there is really a market for its product. It needs to find out how people would react to the new phone.

Ad hoc or continuous?

1. Cross-sectional.

2. Longitudinal – the gym needs to track the performance of users of the different types of classes over time.

3. Cross-sectional.

4. Cross-sectional.

Creating a research design: case study

One possible research design would be to have three stages:

1. Qualitative research among current customers of T H Stores. The objectives of this stage would be:
   a. To determine what types of products customers feel are lacking in stores in the area.
   b. To determine which of these types of products customers would feel happy to buy from T H Stores, and whether they would be consistent with what the store currently sells.
   c. To explore the importance of the family-friendly atmosphere of T H Stores and whether changes in that or loss of it would cause current customers to stop using T H Stores.

2. Qualitative research among people who shop in the area but do not currently use T H Stores. The objectives of this stage would be:
   a. To determine what types of products these people feel are lacking in stores in the area.
   b. To determine which of these types of products these people would feel happy to buy from T H Stores.
   c. To explore their perceptions of T H Stores, and why they do not currently use it.

3. Quantitative research among people who shop in the area. The aim of the research would be to find out which of the products suggested by the qualitative research would be the most appropriate for T H Stores to sell. This stage could investigate:
   a. How likely respondents would be to buy these products from T H Stores.

b. How many current customers would be likely to stop using T H Stores if the atmosphere changed.

c. How many new customers would be attracted into T H Stores if the product range was extended and the atmosphere changed.

The two qualitative stages could run concurrently, but the quantitative stage must follow these as it needs to use the information from the qualitative research.

From this research programme, estimates of additional business can be made and compared against the cost of expansion to determine whether or not it would be worthwhile.

Chapter 4: Research methodologies

Data collection: methods check

1. Postal survey

2. CAPI

3. Internet survey

4. CATI

Methods matching: revision task

1. C

2. D

3. G

4. F

5. A

6. E

7. B

Collecting data: case study

The research design proposed two stages of qualitative research, and one of quantitative research.

Qualitative research – discussion groups

Group discussions would be useful for this stage. The researcher wants to uncover shared knowledge and generate ideas about products that are not well catered for in the area. She also wants to find out about the views currently held about T H Stores. Discussion groups could deliver a lot of information and ideas in a short time.

Quantitative research – in-street interviews

The aim is to interview people who shop in the area, so the most cost-effective way is to interview in the streets around the store. The researcher could use either CAPI or pen and paper, but would not use a self-completion questionnaire because of the difficulties of both giving them out and collecting them in from people on the street.

Chapter 5: Sampling

Identifying the population of interest

1. Current customers. The research needs to investigate how current customers feel.

2. Residents in the area covered by the recycling scheme: they can inform the council about how much they use the scheme, and what they think of it.

   People who work on the scheme (eg those who collect or dispatch the recycled waste): they will be able to give information on how much waste is collected, which streets recycle most etc.

3. Customers who come into the shops and cafés: these people already buy the company's products. It is important to find out how they will react to the new flavours.
   People who do not normally visit the shops or cafés. They can help the company find out whether the new flavours will help create 'new' customers.
   Staff in the shops and cafés: they will be able to give information about the most popular flavours, how customers combine flavours etc.

Random sampling: methods check

1. Interval sampling: Every fifth house has been selected, starting at Number 4.

2. Simple random sampling: five houses have been chosen at random.

3. Stratified random sampling: there are two clear groups we need to sample from. The households with two or fewer children outnumber those with three or more in a ratio of 4:1. We need four houses with two or fewer children, and one with three or more. This is proportional stratified random sampling.

Selecting the best sample: case study

Option 1
There are four possible groups here:

1. Current customers, who include the 'solo purchasers', children, mothers and families.

2. People who don't currently shop at T H Stores.

3. Local council.

4. Suppliers.

Group 1 could be selected by *quota* from people who come into the store.

Group 2 could be selected in the local area by recruiters, using a short screening questionnaire.

Groups 3 and 4: this is likely to be a very small group. Judgement or convenience sampling are likely to be most useful.

Option 2
The population of interest is the same for Option 1. Groups 1 and 2 could be selected by quota. However, it will be difficult to gather quantitative data from Groups 3 and 4. This is because each is very small. Views of these groups could be gathered by depth interviews.

Chapter 6: Using quantitative research methods

Carrying out interviews

1. In-street interviews.

2. Telephone interviews used to carry out an opinion poll.

3. A hall test, used to carry out a taste test.

4. In-home interviews.

Self-completion questionnaires

1. Postal survey.

2. Customer satisfaction survey.

3. Online questionnaire (or CAWI).

4. Omnibus survey (this is also a postal survey as questionnaires must be returned by post).

Collecting quantitative data practice task – suggested approaches

1. Kitchen Gadgets: an *online questionnaire* would be an easy way of contacting customers who buy online. This option would also allow the company to show pictures of the new range to the respondents.

2. Local health authority: *in-home interviews* would be useful for this project. Asking questions about people's health and related issues can be very sensitive, and being interviewed in their home might make them feel more relaxed. This would also allow the interviewer to show the respondents the sample educational material.

3. If T H Stores has CCTV, it can set up an *observation* project to look at how people move through the store. There might be areas that seem hidden to the customers, and the film footage could help identify these. T H Stores could also set up some *in-store interviews* to find out how aware their customers are about the layout of the shop.

Chapter 7: Using qualitative research methods

Depth interviews or discussion groups?

1. Discussion groups would help to generate ideas for the aftershave.

2. Individual interviews are likely to be the most appropriate here. Mental illness is a very private, sensitive subject and sufferers may not wish to talk in a group. However, discussion groups could be an option for those who wish to share their experience.

3. Duos or trios might be useful here. Different groups of employees might share equipment in different ways and interviewing some of these small groups of 'sharers' you can get insight into these differences.

Encouraging respondents to talk

1. Projective technique, focusing on brand personality.

2. Pieces of fabric being used as stimulus material.

3. The audio recording is the stimulus material for a word association task.

4. Collage to represent the respondents' feelings about the car.

Developing a topic guide: case study

The following stages might be included in the topic guide:

Introduction – to clarify purpose of the research and get to know the respondents:

- Give respondents information about the aim of the research, the length of the discussion and how the information will be used – check they understand and agree. Confirm that all information will be anonymous.

- Ask for background information: who they are, how close to the shop they live, how often they shop there. What goods do they think they can't buy in the area that they would like to be able to?

Reasons for choosing T H Stores – to build an understanding of their current habits and opinions:

- Why do they shop there? What do they like/dislike? Where else do they shop?

- How do their other choices compare with T H Stores?

Changes to the store – to help gather ideas to inform the development:

- What would encourage them to shop only at T H Stores?

- What should be included in the new store?

- What different areas would they like? (Respondents can draw this.)

- Why would their suggestions improve the store?

- Of the things that they earlier said they would like to be able to buy, which would be appropriate for T H Stores to sell?

Closing section:

- What was the best idea they heard during the discussion? (Helps to measure popularity of suggestions.)

- Are there any other ideas they would like to suggest?

- Remind the respondents how the data will be used, and that all information will be anonymous.

Chapter 8, Designing the questionnaire

Getting the question right

1. The question asks about range and usefulness, so there are two questions in one here. Also, it is likely that respondents will say 'fairly satisfied' or 'quite satisfied'. The question needs a scale of responses.

2. This is very complex wording for quite a simple question. Also, it is unclear what is meant by 'near future'. Some respondents might think this means 'a few weeks' and others 'a few months'. Giving a specific time period (eg six months) would be more appropriate.

3. This is a very complex question, as it asks people to agree with a negative statement. It is quite difficult to decide what they are being asked to agree or disagree with. Also, there is no option to disagree given in the question.

Labelling the questionnaire

1. Question 7 (a yes/no question).

2. Questions 6 and 8 (the interviewer must not read out the list of newspaper titles).

3. Following Question 7 (If 'Yes', go to Question 8. If 'No', go to Question 9).

4. Numbers in square brackets, eg [1], following each question.

Designing a questionnaire: case study

Problems include:

■ Poor ordering of questions: The specific questions about T H Stores come before the more general question about where the respondent shops.

■ There are no interviewer instructions or routing instructions. Where should respondents go if they answer 'Never' to Question 9?

■ All the possible responses in Question 10 are very positive, but it is not known whether the respondent does like shopping there.

■ There are no options to say 'don't know' or express an 'other' opinion in questions 10 and 11.

■ Questions 10 and 12 are very leading. It's clear for Question 12 that the questioner wants a positive answer.

Chapter 9: Analysing research data

Data types practice task

1. Nominal

2. Nominal

3. Ordinal

4. Ratio

5. Interval

Chapter 10: Reporting and communicating findings

Preparing to communicate findings

The Italian-based company has commissioned a UK-based research agency. A number of questions need to be asked when the reporting stage is being planned, including:

- The language of the written report. Does the client want the report to be produced in English or Italian – or both languages?

- Presenting the information. Where will presentations take place? Will the researchers need to go to Italy for the presentation, or would the client be happy with a video presentation? Which language should be used for the presentation?

- Making sure that the context is clear. How well does the client understand the UK designer clothing market? The report and/or presentation may need to give some focus to the differences between the UK and Italian markets.

- Suggestions for next steps. What does this information tell the client about opportunities in the UK and what might be done next? What guidance or recommendations can the research agency give?

The research agency needs to make sure that the client understands exactly what the information means in the context of the UK, and what options are given by the research findings.

Organizing information for maximum impact

- What is the size of the sample for each of the groups (boys and girls in Year 1 and in Year 2)? This information should be shown below the table.

- Create separate tables for results from boys and those from girls to make comparison easier.

- Decide on a format for the percentages. All should be given with the same number of decimal places. Rounding to one decimal place is possibly the best option.

Presenting the findings: case study

Some areas to discuss include:

■ Who is going to attend the presentation, and how do they view the project? Find out as much as possible about the possible reactions ahead of time.

■ Are there any findings that the contact feels should be stressed? S/he might have a clearer insight into the owners' level of understanding of the project.

■ What are the practical constraints? Think about how much time there will be, what the room is like, what the owners will be doing immediately before/after the presentation. The last point is important because it might dictate how much attention they can give to the presentation.

■ What resources are available? For example, is the room equipped with a projector?

■ Are there any recommendations that should be highlighted? How much support will the owners need to help turn findings into action?

Test questions answer guide

Question	Answer	For more information, see
1	A	Chapter 2
2	D	Chapter 2
3	B	Chapter 3
4	A	Chapters 4 and 7
5	B	Chapter 5
6	C	Chapter 3
7	C	Chapters 4, 6 and 8
8	D	Chapter 7
9	A	Chapter 7
10	D	Chapter 5
11	A	Chapter 5
12	B	Chapter 6
13	B	Chapter 6
14	C	Chapters 6 and 7
15	D	Chapter 7
16	A	Chapter 8
17	D	Chapter 8
18	C	Chapter 9
19	B	Chapter 9
20	C	Chapter 11

References

AQR (2002) *Qualitative Research Recruitment: Best practice – rules and guidelines* [Online] www.aqr.org.uk (accessed 16 June 2006)

Birn, R (2000) *International Handbook of Market Research Techniques*, Kogan Page, London

Brace, I (2004) *Questionnaire Design*, Kogan Page, London

ESOMAR (1995) ICC/ESOMAR International Code of Marketing and Social Research Practice [Online] www.esomar.org/web/show/id=43240 (accessed 16 June 2006)

Market Research Society (MRS) (2004) *Market Research: An introduction* (training programme) [Online] www.mrs.org.uk/training/online.htm (accessed 16 June 2006)

MRS (2005a) *Code of Conduct* [Online] www.mrs.org.uk/standards/downloads/code2005.pdf (accessed 16 June 2006)

MRS (2005b) *Responsibilities of Interviewers* [Online] www.mrs.org.uk/standards/downloads/revised/active/responsibilities_interviewers_2005.pdf (accessed 16 June 2006)

Social Research Association (SRA) (2003) *Ethical Guidelines*[Online] www.the-sra.org.uk/documents/pdfs/ethics03.pdf (accessed 16 June 2006)

Index

design stages   88–95
  flow   91–92
  incomplete   66
  information collection   34–36, 66–69,
    87–99
  information objectives   88–89
  labelling   94
  logic   91, 92
  omnibus surveys   67–68
  piloting   94–95
  practice task   69
  response rates   35, 68
  satisfaction questionnaires   35, 66
  self-completion   34–36, 66–69, 90,
    93
  user-friendly layout   93
questions
  appropriate   89–91
  classification   92
  content   89
  dichotomous   90
  general to specific   91–92
  open-ended   34, 104
  practice task   91
  pre-coded   90, 93, 104
  prompted/unprompted   90, 91
  routing   93
  spontaneous   91–92
  structured questions   34–36
  types   89–90
  wording   89
quota sampling   55–56, 66

radio frequency identifier tags (RFIDs)   38
random-digit dialling (RDD)   63
random route sampling   56
random sampling
  cluster   53
  inapplicable   53
  interval sampling   52
  methodology   51–54
  multi-stage   53, 56
  recycling scheme   52
  simple   52
  stratified   52
recruiters, discussion groups   40

reliability   48
research
  agencies   7, 11
  awareness   10
  brief   16–18
  findings   117–27
  meaning   4
  reports   123–25
  researchers   6–8, 15, 128–32
  suppliers   6–7
Research Buyer's Guide (RBG)   8, 10, 63,
  78, 129, 131
research design
  case study   28
  creation   25–27
  descriptive research   23, 26
  exploratory   23, 26
  information needs   19–25
  practice   26–27
  selection   19–29
  time-frame   24–25
research objectives
  case study   15
  definition   12–18
  hypothesis   14
  information   88–89, 111, 113
research projects
  ad hoc   24, 25
  budgets/costs   16, 17, 27, 49, 58, 64
  continuous   25
  cross-sectional research   24–25
  deadlines   16, 17
  design   19–29
  existing information   13–14, 20, 26,
    31–33
  feasibility   14
  first steps   12–13
  research brief   16–18
  research proposals   16
  resources   15–16
research proposals
  binding contract   27
  competitive document   27
  drafting   28
  research design   16
  working plan   27